MOVING TO NAPLES

THE UN-TOURIST GUIDE

ALYSIA SHIVERS

To my mom & dad, who always encouraged me to spread my wings and fly, no matter how far away from their nest.

And to my husband, Weston, who I feel blessed every day to call mine.

CONTENTS

INTRODUCTION

NAPLES IS MUCH MORE THAN JUST BEACHES AND SUNSHINE

On the surface, Naples, Florida is a beautiful beachside town. And yet, for a town of its size, Naples has so much more to offer than what vacationers' untrained eyes behold. The beach is just one of the dozens of reasons Naples continues to attract new residents of all ages. For those who live, work and play in this Gulf Coast paradise, the area's low cost of living and slower pace of life actually trump Naples' more popular hallmarks, like the beach. Yes, you read that correctly. Naples is (gasp!) affordable.

Source: Mike Dodge

Does this surprise you? Many perceive Naples to be an exclusive retreat for the wealthy, but regular folks are finding that living here is actually considerably cheaper than other areas of the country. The most touted advantage to life in Naples is the absence of a state income tax, but did you also know that property taxes, energy costs and housing in Naples take less of a bite out of your budget compared to many northern locales?

Additionally, if you're coming to Naples from a big city, like Washington, D.C., Chicago, Dallas, or San Francisco, you will surely notice a slower pace of life here, not to mention roads that are much less congested. Rush hour here is like driving at midnight on the Beltway around D.C.

This combination of perks encourages many folks to move here.

14 REASONS TO CALL NAPLES HOME

Here is a quick look at the top 14 reasons to live in Naples:

Reason No. 1
Wonderful Weather

Source: Scott Kelsey

Imagine never having to pick up a snow shovel again. Why endure those long, gray days of winter that hang around for months up north, while here in Southwest Florida we wake to sunshine every day? There's just no comparison. Naples experiences California-like weather during winter. While our summers are hot and humid, we simply rely on a little invention called air conditioning to make those sultry days bearable. Plus, we are regularly cooled by a comfortable sea breeze.

Reason No. 2
Low Cost of Living

Many people perceive that the costs of housing and energy, not to mention property taxes, in Naples are astronomical. This is a myth. In reality, the typical residential monthly electric bill is $94.72, according to Florida Power & Light (based on 1,000 kWh, in July 2012). Compare that to $128.40 in Michigan, $154.68 in New York, and $203.91 in California.

And then there's housing: $350,000 will buy you a spacious three-bedroom, two-bath home, often with a pool or a view or both, in Naples, but it will barely enable you to buy a one-room, closet-sized apartment in Manhattan, a cozy two-bedroom condo in Chicago, where you'd also have to shell out an additional $30,000 for a parking spot, or a 1960s, two-bedroom ranch with about 1,000 square feet of living space in Napa, California. Property taxes in California, New York and New Jersey will bleed you dry, while in Naples they amount to approximately 1.2% of your home's value.

Reason No. 3
Wide Variety of Housing

While the mega-mansions along the beaches are an amazing spectacle, that level of wealth represents just a small slice of Naples life. Naples offers housing for every lifestyle and every budget. Choose from charming beach cottages, towering beachfront condominiums, custom architectural masterpieces, contemporary single-family homes, condos, villas, and carriage and town homes in gated, master-planned communities; expansive horse farms, and manufactured homes.

Reason No. 4
Abundant Educational Opportunities – From Pre-K to MBA

The educational selection in Naples spans from offerings for the youngest learners, in preschool, to programs geared toward those seeking advanced degrees. The Collier County Public Schools has expanded as the area's population has grown, placing schools at every corner of the county and everywhere in between. If you're seeking a private-school environment, Naples has some highly regarded ones. Charter schools are also starting to gain a foothold in Naples. College choices include Hodges University and Edison State College, which are in town, as

Source: Edison State College

well as <u>Florida Gulf Coast University</u>, which is just a 30-minute drive away.

Reason No. 5
Excellent Health Care

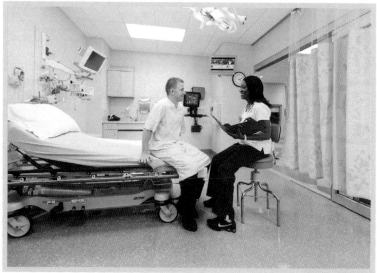

With highly rated, skilled physicians and surgeons who have a broad range of specialties, and plenty of walk-in clinics, Naples offers a wealth of health-care options. <u>NCH Healthcare System</u> has two hospitals with a total of 715 beds. NCH is also home to the Naples Heart Institute, a dedicated pediatric unit, and the <u>Brookdale Center for Healthy Aging and Rehabilitation</u>.

<u>Physicians Regional Healthcare</u> System also has two hospitals that provide extensive specialist services, including cardiology, oncology, gastrointestinal care, obstetrics, and pediatrics.

Naples residents also benefit from a plethora of doctors in every specialty imaginable. In addition to references from friends and colleagues, sites like http://www.Healthgrades.com will help guide you to the best local physician.

Reason No. 6
Midwestern Friendliness

The people of Naples are a friendly bunch. And why wouldn't we be? We get to live in paradise every day. You'll meet people here from every corner of the globe and they are happy to extend a friendly greeting to those who have just found Naples. No matter where you started out, you are sure to find someone here from your home state, maybe even your hometown. We all were new to Naples once!

Reason No. 7
Unlimited Outdoor Activities

The list of outdoor activities here is endless. From tennis and baseball to biking and golf, the Naples outdoors is your sporting paradise. Nearly every community offers some sort of recreation area; and, if you can't find what you're looking for, you can go to one of the many county parks where ball fields, racquetball courts and walking trails await. With what's been reported as the most holes per capita, it's no surprise that golf is one of our most popular activities.

Gareth Rockliffe

Reason No. 8
The Beach and Beyond

Water is everywhere in Naples, from canals and backwater bays to the Gulf of Mexico itself, making boating, kayaking, canoeing, paddle boarding and fishing all popular activities. The endless stretches of Naples beaches are open to the public. In the city of Naples, every road from 7th Avenue North to 18th Avenue South ends at the beach, offering residents and visitors plenty of parking spaces. Up in North Naples, you'll find parking garages, county parks and a state park that provide access to the beaches. Residents even get free beach parking stickers from the county.

Reason No. 9
The Wildlife

An extraordinary range of wildlife flourishes here in Southwest Florida. The birds alone, from the ibis to the blue heron to the anhinga, are amazing creatures, but the area is also known for its alligators, panthers and tortoises. Though it's rare that you'll cross paths with some of these animals unless you're at an area attraction, it's nice to know the creatures who share our land.

Reason No. 10
Year-Round Flowers and Greenery

Forget gray and gloomy northern winters where the grass is brown and the trees are bare for half the year. In Naples, no matter what side of the bed you happen to wake up on, what a pleasure it is to look outside and be surrounded by a lush landscape. Trees remain green and palms flourish year-round. Heavenly Hibiscus, beautiful Bougainvillea, and dozens more flowering plants brighten our landscape twelve months a year. We even boast landscaped medians that make driving along Naples' roadways a pleasant experience.

Reason No. 11
So Many Restaurants

No matter what you're craving or what you want to pay, you'll find just the right Naples restaurant to please your palette and your budget. High-end, low-end, fast food, fine dining, pizza parlors, fish houses, romantic rendezvous, family-style eateries, healthy alternatives, and waterfront cafes are all here. With more than 400 restaurants in Naples, you could eat at a different one every night for a year and still not hit them all.

Reason No. 12
Entertainment and Attractions

Source: Scott Kelsey

Living in a vacation area has its perks. Whether you're out for the day with the kids, your partner or a group of friends, Naples has plenty to do and see. The area has its own zoo, botanical garden, philharmonic center, art and history museums, sightseeing cruises, and water parks. Plus, Everglades National Park is right in our backyard. Full-time residents can feel like tourists whenever the mood strikes because an event or an attraction is always begging to be discovered.

Reason No. 13
Shopping, Shopping and More Shopping

As a relatively small town, Naples has a surprising abundance of shopping choices, from Saks and Nordstrom to Walmart and Costco. We benefit from the many malls, strip plazas, boutiques, outlets, galleries and outdoor promenades boasting high-end retailers. You'll also find a unique collection of independent stores.

Reason No. 14
Lots of Arts, Culture and Music

Given its reputation as a world-class destination, Naples attracts some big-name talent to Artis—Naples (formerly the Philharmonic of Naples), Naples Museum of Art, and Germain Arena. Your calendar is sure to be full year-round with musical acts, gallery viewings, comedy shows and more.

CHAPTER 1

A VERY BRIEF HISTORY OF NAPLES

From Pre-History to Today

Humans have populated the Naples area for thousands of years. But, until very recently, the only residents were the Calusa Indians who wandered freely throughout Southwest Florida.

By the mid-1800s, humans had vanished and only a rich variety of wildlife – from pelicans to panthers and from osprey to otters – remained.

Naples, Florida, Is Established in the Late 1800s

Naples was still full of plant and animal life, but devoid of human beings, until a schooner arrived in 1885 off the coast of what is now the city of Naples.

That schooner carried one of the founders of Naples, Walter N. Haldeman, from Louisville, Kentucky. He actually picked the spot that was to become Naples.

The new settlement was never a fishing village; Naples was always intended to be a warm, healthy winter getaway, according to Haldeman's granddaughter, Florence Haldeman Price:

> *"Grandfather definitely sought a healthy winter home for his family: sunshine, warmth and outdoor living. He wanted it on the mainland, washed by waters of the Gulf. He did not want an island. And that mainland is what he found."* (Source: When Peacocks Were Roasted and Mullet Was Fried)

The name "Naples" was given to the nascent town to suggest that this wonderful wilderness would one day become just as beautiful, sophisticated, and desirable as Naples, Italy. In 1888, that vision was still a dream and our Naples had just 80 residents.

Source: Collier County Museums

In 1889, the first, 16-room, Naples hotel and the municipal pier were built. They were connected by a rustic wooden walkway that allowed for the movement of people, luggage, and supplies.

Arriving always by boat, intrepid winter visitors filled the hotel, which became the center of the tiny town's social life for decades to come. Today's Naples Beach Hotel is a direct descendent of that rustic resort.

Collier County Roots Planted in 1911

While the growth of the city of Naples proceeded at a glacial pace into the early 20th century, Baron Gift Collier, a wealthy advertising tycoon from New York City separately discovered what was to become Collier County in 1911. He soon fell in love:

> *"Frankly, I was fascinated with Florida and swept off my feet by what I saw and felt," he once explained. "It was a wonder land with a magic climate, set in a frame of golden sunshine." – from the Collier County Museums biography of Collier*

That love of Florida, combined with a sense of limitless possibility, inspired him to purchase more than one million acres of wilderness. Much of that wilderness became Collier County, stretching from the Gulf of Mexico into The Everglades. Barron Collier ultimately drove the creation of the Tamiami Trail from Fort Myers to Miami.

It was not until the 1920s that Naples and Collier County officials began developing the infrastructure to support future growth. In fact, no paved roads existed before 1923 and electricity didn't come along until 1926. Travelers had no easy way to get from Naples to Miami, a mere 120 miles across the state, until the Tamiami Trail was completed in 1928.

The 1920s brought plenty of modernization, but by 1930, just 390 residents called Naples home.

Real Growth Comes After World War II

The most significant growth came after World War II, beginning in the 1950s.

In 1950, Naples got its first bank. Before then, a drive to Fort Myers was necessary. Naples' first hospital wasn't built until 1955.

Ironically, Hurricane Donna in 1960 spurred an amazing building boom, thanks to $25 million in insurance payments to owners of destroyed properties. Construction boomed as homes, offices, and hotels were rebuilt.

Source: Naples Beach Hotel

Typical Neapolitan resilience was displayed by Naples Beach Hotel Owner Henry Watkins Sr., who said, *"We'll just build it back better."* In fact, the hotel reopened just a month after the hurricane. And, as Naples grew, so did the Naples Beach Hotel. As the city moved into the 21st century, the Watkins family continued to invest in the hotel with the addition of gracious rooms, extensive meeting space, and sophisticated tennis facilities.

Explosive Growth Begins in the 1980s

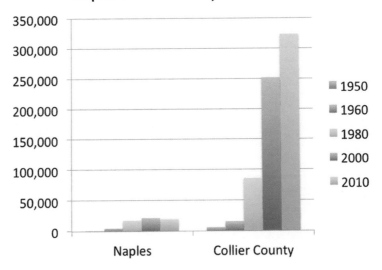

POPULATION GROWTH
Naples & Collier County: 1950 to 2010

Many more hotels arose along the Gulf, but the area's true growth accelerator was almost certainly the opening of the Ritz-Carlton Hotel in 1985. Suddenly, Naples was luring thousands of corporate CEOs and wealthy entrepreneurs to newly built luxury Gulf-front condominiums and palatial homes and villas in planned communities that stretched from the Gulf to many miles inland.

The word was out. By the 1990s, new residents from all income levels flocked to the now-booming greater Naples community. Collier County had grown from 85,971 residents in 1980 to 251,377 residents in 2000—and to 322,739 by 2010. That's almost as large as the city of Cleveland, Ohio, from which many Naples residents migrated.

Naples is no longer a sleepy little paradise known to just a fortunate few. Today, it is a sophisticated small city that offers a warm climate and a warm welcome to brand-new residents attracted from all over the world.

CHAPTER 2

QUICK GEOGRAPHIC GUIDE TO NAPLES

Naples lies within Collier County, the largest county in all of Florida, encompassing approximately 2,305 square miles. Naples addresses make up a large portion of Collier County; however, only an itsy-bitsy section is designated as the City of Naples. The City of Naples is the area from Port Royal north to Pine Ridge Road and east from the Gulf of Mexico to Goodlette-Frank Road, between Golden Gate Parkway and the Riverwalk area. Those who live within the limits of the City of Naples pay a bit more in taxes for the privilege, but the services provided, from maintenance to security, are well worth it.

Naples' main east-to-west thoroughfares are Immokalee Road, Pine Ridge Road, Vanderbilt Beach Road, Golden Gate Parkway, and Davis Boulevard. Its main north-to-south thoroughfares are Goodlette-Frank Road, Airport-Pulling Road, Livingston Road, Logan Boulevard/ Santa Barbara Boulevard, and Collier Boulevard/951. Tamiami Trail, also known as U.S. 41, and Interstate 75 connect Naples with Miami and Tampa.

North Naples

No defining line indicates that you have arrived in North Naples, but those who live there are quick to point out proudly that they do indeed live in North Naples. Primarily located around Pine Ridge Road, north to Immokalee Road, North Naples is appealing because of its highly rated schools, as well as its many conveniences, including Whole Foods, Trader Joe's, Super Target, Costco, Sam's Club, and the popular shopping and dining destinations known as Mercato and Waterside Shops. North Naples' popularity and growth happened as the result of a natural population movement toward the north as Old Naples, which encompasses the southern portion of the area, and sections of East Naples, were built out. Suddenly, an area of town that once seemed so far away from civilization became the place to be. Lined with many gated communities, its highly traveled roads have been widened to three lanes in each direction to handle the influx of people. The bonus of residing in this popular part of town is that "newer" amenities and conveniences are all within minutes of your home.

Old Naples

The traditional heart of Naples is Old Naples. Here you'll find winding streets and avenues lined with beautiful banyan trees. Most of the streets end right at the beach. Many original beach cottages still exist, but just as many have been razed to make way for larger, more modern residences. Neighborhoods like The Moorings, Park Shore and Coquina Sands exist here and they are not gated. In fact, Port Royal, Naples' most expensive and most exclusive community, is in this part of town and, while its residents have pushed to gate it, it remains accessible to all. The result is a steady stream of tourists driving very slowly

through the community, gawking at the huge mansions that line Port Royal's roads. Old Naples is home to 5th Avenue South and Third Street South, areas known for their shopping and dining options, as well as Tin City and Bayfront.

Gulfshore Boulevard and Gulf Shore Drive

Source: Mike Dodge

These two stretches of roads are lined with towering condominiums that directly overlook the beaches. Location alone makes this area a desirable one, but you must want to live the condo lifestyle to be right on the beach. Many of the buildings are gated and they pamper their residents with endless amenities, including private parks and an elevated walkway along the dunes. For those living along Gulfshore Boulevard, the Village on Venetian Bay offers unique shopping and dining opportunities set along the calm bay waters.

Pelican Bay

One of the more notable master-planned communities in Naples, Pelican Bay encompasses more than five square miles, which is why many of its residents consider Pelican Bay to be a town of its own. Every type of housing style exists here, as well as a 27-hole golf course. Residents have access to a private beach on the Gulf of Mexico, and the community is anchored by Artis – Naples (formerly Naples Philharmonic Center for the Arts) and Waterside Shops.

East and South Naples

These areas of Naples, which primarily fall along the Radio Road, Davis Boulevard, Golden Gate Parkway and Collier Boulevard corridors, are home to several communities: some gated, some not, some with golf, others with beautiful lakes and nature preserves. All offer quick access to Old Naples and the beaches. Here you'll find Naples Airport, where, particularly during high season, you'll see many private jets flying in and out. Edison State College and the Collier County government complex are also based here.

Golden Gate Estates

Situated east of the north-south corridor, Collier Boulevard, also referred to as 951, is Golden Gate Estates, a huge expanse of Collier County that was developed when thousands of one-acre-plus parcels were sectioned off. This area is attractive to those who desire land, be it for raising livestock, stabling horses, storing boats and RVs, or simply for privacy. Deed restrictions do not exist here and no association exists to tell you how to maintain your property; thus, residents do not pay homeowners association fees. For those who prefer the freedom to do as they please on their land – within legal boundaries of course! – and who prefer owning more than a typical quarter-acre lot, the

Estates will appeal to you. Going farther east does put you farther away from conveniences, though. Gas and groceries are not easy to come by and usually require a trip into town. For example, approximately 10 miles separates Everglades Boulevard from the closest Publix grocery store on 951.

Getting Around Town

Naples' vast network of roads, abundant parking, and limited public transportation, make car ownership a requirement for many residents. Some communities have everything you might need – grocery stores, restaurants, retail shops – within walking or biking distance, but a car is a necessity, generally, when it comes to getting around town.

Source: Mike Dodge

If you're traveling around Naples by car, the roads are easy to navigate and generally follow a basic grid pattern. Because so many of our communities are gated, most traffic is forced out onto the main arteries. Back roads are limited here.

Be extra cautious when driving around town. With the ample number of tourists and snowbirds that fill our roads during the winter and early spring, it is not unusual for drivers to be slow and distracted as they take in the sights.

For those who don't want the fuss of owning a car, the county does provide bus transportation via Collier Area Transit (CAT).

These big green and white buses travel countywide and now include a route that links Collier with the county to our north, Lee County. The buses operate seven days a week. Bus schedules and fees are available by visiting www.colliergov.net.

Maybe a bicycle is your preferred mode of transportation? If so, you'll be happy to know that Naples is a very bike-friendly town, with designated bike lanes on its roads.

Taxi service is available, but it can be expensive, especially if you're just out with friends enjoying the Naples restaurant scene. A new service, Jump On Express, or JOE, for short, offers a great alternative for weekend restaurant hopping. Running from 6 p.m. to 2 a.m. on Thursdays, Fridays and Saturdays, JOE stops at Mercato, Fifth Avenue South and Third Street South every 30 minutes, giving you and your friends the opportunity to circulate among the town's three hot spots free of charge.

CHAPTER 3

FLORIDA SEASONS

Naples has two seasons: the dry season and the rainy season.

Fall and Winter

During the fall and winter months, the area sees very little, if any, rain, and the temperatures are comfortable during the day and can be a bit chilly overnight. According to The Weather Channel, our lowest recorded temperature was 26 degrees in January 1982. We got pretty close to that record in December 2010, when the temperature dropped to 27 degrees. We can, and do, get frost, which jeopardizes our citrus crops, and longtime residents report that snowflakes *have* fallen in Naples.

January is typically the coolest month, but the whole of winter, from November through March, consists of lows averaging around 50 degrees and highs averaging in the 70s. Sometime in mid- to late-October, the humidity clicks off, which is, occasionally, a teaser and lasts only for a few days. Eventually, though, the humidity ends for good and Naples enjoys months of fantastic weather that allows you to turn off the air conditioning, open the windows, and you'll even drag a light jacket out from the back of the closet once in a while.

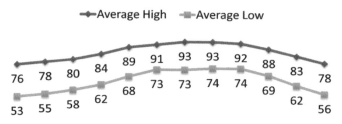

Average Naples Temperatures

Jan Feb Mar Apr May Jun Jul Aug Sep Oct Nov Dec

On those rare nights when the weatherman calls for temperatures in the 30s, you may even turn on the heat. Just don't be surprised if the smoke detectors go off. Dust has accumulated on the coils and the air will smell scorched for a few moments. If you don't find the need to turn on the heat over the course of a winter season, it might be best to do so anyway just to burn off that accumulated dust.

The Gulf of Mexico also gets chilly over the winter. Depending on how long some of our cold spells last, the water temperature can easily drop into the 50s.

At the beach, it's easy to pick out the residents and the tourists. Residents are walking the beach in shorts or pants and a long-sleeved shirt. Tourists are happily splashing around in the cold water.

Spring and Summer

Summer is Naples' rainy season, better known as hurricane season. Typically, we start to see the rains return around May, but by June our regular afternoon thunderstorms are in full force. Naples sees an average of eight to ten inches of rain every June, July, August and September, according to The Weather Channel. The thunderstorms here are something to see. If you happen to be driving, you can look down the road and what appears to be haze ahead is, in fact, a wall of water. The clouds are amazing to watch as they roll in and bring stunning lightning shows and loud thunder. It's not unusual to see rain in the front of your community and dry air in the back; or the sky in North Naples might look black as night, but the sun is shining brightly in Old Naples.

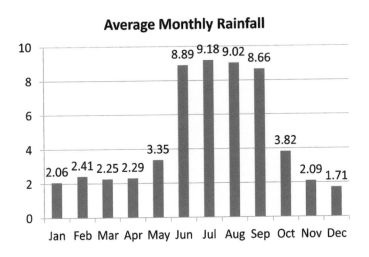

And with the summer rains come the humidity.

Spring and summer months are when you'll find yourself sweating the instant you walk outside, without even exerting yourself. Just like in Washington, D.C., Houston, Las Vegas and Phoenix, Neapolitans spend a lot of time in air-conditioned places during the summer, whether at home, in restaurants, shops, or movie theaters. If we do go outside, it's usually first thing in the morning or just before sunset to walk the dogs, jog or bike around the neighborhood.

What you might find surprising, however, is that Naples has never reached 100 degrees. According to The Weather Channel, the highest recorded temperature was 99 degrees, in September 1986. Of course, when you factor in the humidity, it can feel like 105, but the fact remains that Naples hasn't reached the 100 mark on the thermometer, unlike the oppressive 100-plus degree days sometimes seen in summer in the northeast and the midwest that can last for days at a time.

The Gulf of Mexico also gets warm in the summer, with water temperatures reaching into the high 80s and low 90s. The water isn't exactly refreshing when it gets that warm, but you can easily walk right in.

Those who don't work in air-conditioned buildings don't have the luxury of being in a climate-controlled environment all day during the hot days of summer. As years go by, your body adjusts to the heat and humidity and temperatures that once felt scorching hot to you might not feel so unbearable, but endless stretches of 90-degree days with added humidity take their toll. Use common sense in the heat: drink lots of water to keep yourself hydrated and take frequent breaks from the sun when you can.

The sun's heat is much stronger here. You may have been able to lie in the sun for hours at your former home and turned a little pink, but Naples is much closer to the equator than other parts of the United States, and that means your skin can burn quickly. Take the necessary precautions and wear sunscreen even if you only plan to shop at an outdoor mall.

One positive effect of all the humidity is that it does a world of good for those who suffered from dry skin in northern climates.

The Reality of Hurricanes

Hurricanes are part of the reality of living in Naples, just as earthquakes are to California and tornadoes are to the central United States. Happily, hurricanes are entirely predictable, so you are unlikely to be caught by surprise.

Hurricane season in the Atlantic begins June 1 and ends November 30. Naples has had its share of storms, but has only ever endured a direct hit by a hurricane once, in 1960. However, that doesn't mean residents take these storms lightly. Hurricanes can be hundreds of miles wide and affect several areas over multiple states.

The National Weather Service reports that 73 tropical storms and hurricanes passed within 75 nautical miles of Naples between 1851 and 2004. Fourteen of those were Category Three, one was Category Four, and one was a Category Five.

For someone not familiar with hurricanes, these numbers might sound frightening. But if you take the necessary precautions, you and your family will be safe. The worst-case scenario would require packing up your car and leaving town, maybe even leaving the state. In other cases, you may elect to go to one of the emergency public shelters. Or, if you prefer to ride out the storm at home, depending on its strength, size and point of impact, you'll take the time to properly shutter your windows and doors, you'll stock up on water, gasoline and food, and you'll buy extra propane for your barbecue grill and batteries for your flashlights and radios.

You'll know when and how to start preparing for a hurricane because the local news crews will report until they are blue in the face about an approaching storm. If you don't watch the news, a wealth of information can be found online about hurricane preparation. Visit www.ready.gov/hurricanes. In today's world, where news is at your fingertips, you can always be prepared.

If this is your first storm, it's easy to go into panic mode because you don't know what to expect, but you have no need to panic. Depending on what's headed our way, most employers will give you ample time to prepare your home or to leave town. No one wants to endanger anyone's safety.

The hurricanes that Naples has experienced since 2004 have forced schools, offices and retail stores to close, have produced a ton of rain and significant winds that have taken down trees, and have resulted in power outages for several days. A smart purchase would be a generator because it will keep the food in the refrigerator from spoiling and will power a few oscillating fans or a window air conditioner.

Seasoned Neapolitans take all the necessary precautions, but if the impending storm looks to be mostly rain and wind, rather than a damaging force majeure, it's not unusual to stock up on party supplies and invite the neighbors over to ride out the storm.

CHAPTER 4

CAN YOU LIVE WELL HERE?

The Cost of Housing

It's much less expensive than you might think to live in Naples.

Housing, usually the biggest chunk of your living expenses, is more affordable than it's been in recent history. Prices are 45 percent below where they were at their 2005-2006 peak in the Naples market.

Today, the median sale price for a home in Naples is approximately $226,500 (slightly above the national median, which is $194,900) and the average sale price is $385,897 *(Sunshine Multiple Listing Service as of February 28, 2013)*. Compare that to where Naples' sales prices were in 2008: $284,500 was the median sale price and $500,102 was the average sale price, and, yes, Naples is once again affordable to most.

The closer you get to the beach, the more expensive the homes will be. Additionally, homes within exclusive gated communities, centered on a golf course with a ton of amenities, will also come with a higher price tag and higher association fees. But throughout Naples, plenty of neighborhoods offer a variety of housing styles at affordable price points. A two-bedroom, two-bath condo in a perfectly nice neighborhood can be found for around $150,000, just as a spacious three-bedroom, two-bath single-family pool home can be found for around $350,000. These affordable options are usually only five to ten miles away from the beaches.

Compare these prices to what you can buy around the country:

- $550,000: A one-bedroom condo in downtown Boston

- $700,000: A 1940s two-bedroom home in Los Angeles

- $800,000: Roughly five acres of land to build a home in Far Hills, New Jersey

- $1 million: A three-bedroom home in Washington, D.C that dates back to the 1800s

- $400,000: A newly constructed townhome in Houston, Texas

- $300,000: A two-bedroom condo in downtown Minneapolis

- $650,000: A one-bedroom, one-bath condo in Long Island, New York

Utilities

Costs associated with housing, like electricity, water, sewer and taxes, are also significantly cheaper than the costs for many of our northern counterparts.

Because we use our air conditioning non-stop for months on end, we do heat our pools during the comfortably cooler winter months, and all of our appliances run on electricity, it's easy to assume that our electricity bills must go through the roof each month. And yet, electricity is not that costly.

According to Florida Power & Light, the primary provider of electricity in Naples, a typical residential 1,000 kWh bill during summer[1] is $94.72 per month, which is considerably lower than the national average of $128.29.

Compare this with the same electricity consumption in the summer up north. States like Michigan and Wisconsin report electric bills of $128 per month. New York comes in at $154, Massachusetts at $155, New Jersey at $170 and California at $203.

During the winter months, the average electricity bill in Naples, based on 1,000 kWh, drops to $94.62[2] per month, still lower than the national average which totals $124.31. In Wisconsin, it's $121, Michigan $130, Pennsylvania $131, New York $147, Massachusetts $166, and California $199.

Forbes.com identifies the following cities as the most expensive when it comes to heating bills:

- Boston:$1,924[3] average annually with 35 percent of residents using oil, 47 percent natural gas, 3 percent propane and 12 percent electricity

- Minneapolis:$1,643 with 1 percent using oil, 82 percent natural gas, 3 percent propane and 10 percent electricity

- Washington, D.C.:$1,609 with 6 percent using oil, 54 percent natural gas, 2 percent propane and 36 percent electricity

- Buffalo, NY:$1,591 with 2 percent using oil, 88 percent natural gas, 2 percent propane and 5 percent electricity

- Philadelphia: $1,574 with 19 percent using oil, 60 percent natural gas, 3 percent propane and 16 percent electricity

- Baltimore, MD:$1,568 with 14 percent using oil, 46 percent natural gas, 3 percent propane and 35 percent electricity

- New York, NY:$1,513 with 32 percent using oil, 56 percent natural gas, 1 percent propane and 8 percent electricity

- Cleveland, OH: $1,232 with 2 percent using oil, 83 percent natural gas, 1 percent propane and 11 percent electricity

- Detroit, MI:$1,214 with 0.6 percent using oil, 90 percent natural gas, 3 percent propane and 5 percent electricity

- Denver, CO:$1,176 with 0.1 percent using oil, 80 percent natural gas, 2 percent propane and 16 percent electricity

- St. Louis, MO:$1,146 with 0.6 percent using oil, 68 percent natural gas, 5 percent propane and 24 percent electricity

[1]*Published in November 2012 based on utility rates effective July 2012, Florida Power & Light*

[2]*Published May 2012 based on utility rates effective Winter 2012, Florida Power & Light*

[3]*Average family of four with a 2,100-square-foot house, Forbes.com*

Water bills are also thought to be costly, and, yes, Floridians do tend to use more water per day than the average American. Of the 8,000 gallons of water used per month by the average Collier County public utilities customer, 5,000 is consumed indoors and 3,000 is used outdoors. Because residents get their water from various utilities, rates vary. Also, unless your irrigation water is pulled from a community lake or via a well on your property, your consumption of central water for irrigation purposes is also tacked onto your water bill.

As an example, using the county's central water system for both water and sewer, 8,000 gallons will run you just under $100 per month for an 1,800-square-foot house on a quarter-acre. That's about the same as Boston, Atlanta or Austin. For more information on water usage, restrictions and conservation, visit www.colliergov.net.

Property Tax

The last piece of the cost-analysis puzzle is property taxes. Property tax rates in Collier County are approximately 1.2 percent of a property's value. Who determines your home's value? The county property appraiser does, by taking into account fair-market value, geographic location and how the property is used.

In Naples, a property assessed at $315,000 would pay property taxes roughly equal to $3,300, compared to:

Property Taxes

City, State	Assessed Value	Taxes
Cleveland Heights, Ohio	$243,640	$23,782
Cherry Hill, New Jersey	$422,400	$24,313
Las Vegas, Nevada	$121,314	$3,309
Chicago, Illinois	$67,209	$10,168
Baltimore, Maryland	$385,300	$4,479
Golden Valley, Minnesota	$371,000	$6,945
Horton, Michigan	$206,678	$6,641
Madison, Wisconsin	$407,400	$8,275

(Source: 2011 taxes as per Realtor.com, which pulls information from public records, and/or Multiple Listing Services from the local jurisdiction)

According to Tax-Rates.org, a site that reports the median property tax rate by state, and even by county, Florida ranks 18th out of the 50 states for property taxes as a percentage of the median income. Counties within each state will have higher or lower property tax rates based on a number of factors. For instance, West Chester County in New York reports the highest median property tax in the state, levying an average of $9,003 yearly in property taxes, while Marin County in California is the highest in that state, at $5,500. In Florida, Miami-Dade County comes in as the highest, with an average bill of $2,756.

Naples property taxes are lower than many places, plus, they are cheaper than the county directly to our north. Lee County, home to such popular cities and towns as Estero, Bonita Springs, Fort Myers and Cape Coral, has a property tax rate of approximately 1.5 to 1.7 percent, meaning a property with an assessed value of $289,000 would owe approximately $4,300 in property tax. Two factors that help keep Naples' property taxes low are our higher home values and our higher concentration of second-home owners.

When you buy property in Naples with the intent of making it your permanent home, you are eligible for the Homestead Exemption, which deducts up to $50,000 from the assessed value of your home. Visit www.collierappraiser.com for more specifics on applying for the Homestead Exemption.

Tax Tip: Honorably discharged veterans with a service-related permanent disability are exempt from paying property taxes in Florida. You must be a permanent resident of Florida and the U.S. Department of Veterans Affairs must confirm your disability.

A General Feeling of Safety

Naples is not only a great place to live; it's also a safe place to live.

According to the Collier County Sheriff's Office, of the 67 counties in Florida, only 12 had lower crime rates than Collier in 2011. Unlike Philadelphia, New York, Boston or Detroit, you're not going to turn on the local nightly news and hear report after report of violent, life-threatening crimes.

Many of our communities are surrounded by gates, some even with a 24-hour guard, which provide a sense of security for their residents.

Overall, Naples has a small-town feel, with neighbors and friends looking out for one another. Some neighborhoods have a Neighborhood Watch, but if you live in a community that doesn't, you can contact the Crime Prevention Unit at (239) 252-0700 to find out how to establish one. Or you can simply get to know your neighbors. Neighbors who watch out for one another can prevent crime. If you see something unusual, you can call the non-emergency hotline at (239) 252-9300 and the Sheriff's Office will check it out.

A Network of Hospitals and Medical Offices

Since 2010, Collier County has consistently ranked among the top four healthiest counties out of 67 counties in Florida by the Robert Wood Johnson Foundation. The ranking is based on physical environment, social and economic factors, health behaviors, education, crime rate/law enforcement, and clinical care. That clinical care includes everything from hospitals to walk-in clinics to physicians' offices. Naples has a wealth of healthcare options.

Source: HMA

NCH Healthcare System

NCH has two hospitals. One is located in downtown Naples, off U.S. 41, and the other is in North Naples, off Immokalee Road. With a total of 715 beds, NCH is home to the Naples Heart Institute, The BirthPlace, the Robert and Mariann MacDonald SeaCAREium Pediatric Unit, the Brookdale Center for Healthy Aging and Rehabilitation, and the Jay and Patty Baker Patient Care Tower, as well as several walk-in clinics and outpatient rehabilitation facilities.

NCH is an award-winning healthcare system recognized in *U.S. News & World Report's* Best Hospitals in 2012-13 for gastroenterology, ear, nose and throat, geriatrics, and orthopedics specialties. For eight years in a row, from 2005-2012, it has been the recipient of the HealthGrades Cardiac Care Excellence Award. For nine years in a row, from 2004-2012, it's been ranked among the top five percent in the nation for overall cardiac and cardiology services. It was ranked No. 2

in Florida for cardiology services in 2012 and ranked No. 1 in Florida for coronary interventional procedures for three years in a row, from 2010-2012.

The American Heart Association awarded NCH its Stroke Silver Quality Achievement award in 2013. It's been five-star rated for treatment of stroke eight years in a row, from 2005-2012.

In Collier County, where heart disease is the second-highest cause of death, behind cancer, NCH is doing its part with its Save-A-Heart program, which has a record of stopping heart attacks within 90 minutes of the patient arriving at its cardiac-cath lab.

Source: NCH

"Smart Rooms," 64 in all, have been installed on the top floors of the Baker Tower on the North Naples campus. What is a Smart Room? It utilizes devices and information technology to communicate among patients, family and staff. Electronic boxes, handheld devices and flat-screen TVs relay information so everyone is on the same page regarding treatment, medications, vital signs, medical records, and so much more.

Physicians Regional Healthcare System

Physicians Regional also has two hospitals, one off Pine Ridge Road, just east of Interstate 75, and the other off Collier Boulevard, south of Rattlesnake Hammock Road. The facility off Collier Boulevard is the newest hospital in Collier County and brings much-needed healthcare choices and vital services, like obstetrics and pediatrics, to East Naples.

With more than 300 physicians who are highly recognized in their fields, the new system offers advanced medical care in more than 45 specialties and subspecialties, including cancer, cardiology, dermatology, digestive care, orthopedics, pain management, pediatrics, rehabilitation, ear, nose and throat, endocrinology, rheumatology, stroke, sleep medicine, infectious diseases, kidney disorders, urology, ophthalmology, wound care and women's health.

Source: HMA

For two years in a row, Physicians Regional has been recognized as a top performer on key quality measures by The Joint

Commission, the leading accreditor of healthcare organizations in America, for exemplary performance in using evidence-based clinical processes that are shown to improve care for certain conditions, including heart attack, heart failure, pneumonia, surgical care, children's asthma, stroke and venous thromboembolism, as well as inpatient psychiatric services.

Walk-In Clinics

Doctors' offices can get crowded, particularly during the time of the year when the population in Naples explodes. It's nice to know that if you can't get in to see your regular doctor, various walk-in clinics around town allow you to do just that: walk in. These facilities usually have weekend hours and they also come in handy until you find a doctor you feel comfortable seeing on a regular basis.

Medical Offices

Source: HMA

Naples residents benefit from having a plethora of doctors in every specialty. To find someone you respect and trust with your

49

health, it might be best to get a recommendation from a friend or a co-worker or through your health plan. Otherwise, you can seek information on sites like Healthgrades.com.

If your pocketbook permits it, you may also want to check into one of the many concierge doctors who have popped up in recent years. These doctors charge an annual fee or provide services on a cash-only basis, meaning they don't bill through insurance companies. In exchange, patients typically receive an enhanced level of care. They can be costly, but they offer personal service.

Community Blood Center

Affiliated with the NCH Healthcare System, the Community Blood Center is committed to supplying every hospital in Collier County with life-saving blood products. Donors can give by visiting the Center at its 9th Street location in Naples or by visiting the BloodMobile which makes frequent stops around town. A full calendar of the BloodMobile's upcoming stops is available on the website, www.nchmd.org. Every donation collected here stays here. Quick Tip: Free valet parking is available to all donors who come to the center. Hours are posted online.

Lee County VA Healthcare Center

Though it is located about an hour away, in Cape Coral, this new, 220,000-square-foot facility dedicated to the needs of our veterans and their families is a welcome addition to Southwest Florida. Before this center opened in late 2012, veterans were forced to travel to Tampa to receive care and specialty services. Now, at this new outpatient facility, primary care, mental health, cardiology, eye care, X-ray, ultrasound, orthopedics, dental and so much more are available locally to veterans.

Avow Hospice

Caring for approximately 1,700 terminally ill patients annually, Avow offers both an inpatient facility on its main campus, as well as a home-care program, caring for people in their homes, nursing homes or assisted living communities. Its team consists of about 230 physicians, registered nurses, licensed practical nurses, social workers, bereavement counselors, certified nurse's aides, chaplains, massage therapists, a pediatric team, a Spanish-language team, a certified music therapist and Reiki practitioners. Plus, more than 300 people volunteer their time.

VITAS Innovative Hospice Care

Headquartered in Miami, VITAS operates 45 hospice programs in 16 states and employs nearly 10,000 professionals who care for terminally ill patients daily, primarily in patients' homes, but also in hospitals, nursing homes and assisted living facilities. In Collier County, VITAS has an inpatient hospice unit at Physicians Regional in Naples.

Important Note About Finding a Doctor for your Child

Unless your pediatrician is delivering your baby in Naples, finding a doctor for your child can be challenging. Even with plenty of doctors to choose from, many will only take a certain number of patients. If you are moving here with a young child, know that it could take a bit of time to locate a doctor. The good news is that all of them are well-educated and most of their offices are concentrated around the hospitals.

CHAPTER 5

CHOOSING WHERE IN NAPLES TO LIVE

A Variety of Housing Choices

Housing options in Naples are limitless.

You can find every choice imaginable:

- Town homes, carriage homes and villas, both attached and detached
- Low rises, mid-rises and high rises
- Towering beachfront and bayfront condominiums

52

- Every size and shape of single-family home.

A multitude of lifestyle choices go along with the housing options. Golf is a popular pastime here and a slew of communities in Naples cater to golf enthusiasts, or just those who like to look out their lanais to see endless manicured greens.

If boating is your activity of choice, numerous neighborhoods nestle along the bay and the area's canals and they include boat docks in every homeowner's backyard.

Source: Gareth Rockliffe

Perhaps you enjoy being at the center of it all. If so, you'll be drawn to the Naples residences overlooking main thoroughfares, giving that feel and convenience of city life.

Source: Scott Kelsey

Naples also has communities that surround you in nature, those that exude a country-like setting, and those that place you within walking distance of the beach.

Of course, you can always choose a place right on our precious stretch of sand, so that you can enjoy the sea breeze and hear the sound of the surf when you open your sliding-glass door. Once you've settled on the style of house you prefer and the lifestyle that appeals to you most, you'll have decide if you want to live in a gated or non-gated community. Depending on what you're used to back home, Naples may surprise you with its abundance of gated communities. They are everywhere.

Life in a gated community has its perks. One perk is that it gives residents an added sense of security, particularly if the gatehouse is staffed around the clock. Gated communities also offer an air of exclusivity because only the residents and their guests can gain access to the community.

Gated communities also come with a fair amount of amenities, which typically include an immense clubhouse with a restaurant, a fitness center, a community pool and spa, gathering rooms and more. Some gated communities are centered on a golf course, while others feature huge lakes, peaceful preserves, or a combination of one or all of the above.

Gates do not appeal to everyone, which is why you'll find some attractive non-gated communities throughout Naples. In downtown Naples, Park Shore, The Moorings and Aqualane Shores are very desirable, non-gated neighborhoods; further east you'll find Berkshire Lakes, Lely Resort and Madison Park; and to the north you'll discover Tall Pines, Pinewoods, Willoughby Acres, Victoria Park and Bridge Way Villas, just to name a few. They may feature amenities, too, but often on a smaller scale.

Gates or not, it is wise to inquire about the fees associated with the community. A long list of amenities is appealing, but keep in mind that homeowners association dues will generally reflect the care and maintenance of all those things on the list. Fees can vary drastically by community. For instance, if you buy in a bundled golf community, the golf membership is "bundled" with the home purchase. Everyone in that community  is automatically a member of the golf club, which, in essence, keeps the club dues lower. Other communities give residents the choice of golf membership or social membership, both of which come with their share of entitlements to the various amenities. And still other communities sell a specific form of membership that varies by residence. For example, in Countryside and Glen Eagle, some condos are sold with a social membership, while others come with a golf membership. No switching is allowed. Homeowners associations are either mandatory or voluntary. Mandatory involvement means each homeowner is obligated to follow a set of rules. If the association is voluntary, however, you can choose to pay and stay or not to pay and stay. Some neighborhoods with voluntary associations include Willoughby Acres, Park Shore, The Moorings and Naples Park. If you choose to pay, you get a vote on what happens within the community and those funds are usually put toward the maintenance of the common areas and events.

The State of the Real Estate Market

Naples' reputation as a getaway for the wealthy precedes itself. Yes, we do have our share of multimillion-dollar beachfront estates and condominiums, as well as exclusive communities whose home prices and memberships indulge the affluent. But you should know that you can find residences here to fit every budget.

Nice, well-maintained, albeit older, condos for $150,000 do exist. So do single-family homes for $300,000. Do they exist exactly where you want to live in Naples? Maybe. Maybe not. However, housing in these price points is becoming scarcer as investors and wise buyers claim the good deals.

In 2011-2012, real estate in Naples returned to "normal" levels, meaning prices returned to where they were prior to the bubble of 2005-2006. The sticker shock of the real-estate boom has vanished. As 2012 came to a close, many of Naples' neighborhoods had returned to or came close to being a balanced market. Several areas even showed a shortage of supply, and with the demand for homes still high, prices in these select areas are starting to increase.

Overall, the Naples real-estate market has stabilized. Foreclosures and short sales, while still part of our market, no longer dominate the landscape. The inventory of homes for sale in 2012 hit record-level lows, resulting in multiple offers on residences that were priced correctly and showed well. As 2012 wrapped up, Naples was transitioning from a buyer's market to a buyer's and a seller's market. Opportunities could be had by all.

Websites like Zillow, Trulia and Realtor.com will show you "real time" property values, but it is always best to talk to a Naples Realtor to get the scoop on what's really going on in the market.

In Naples, home prices reflect location and lifestyle. Whether it's because of the school district or a proximity to newer, more popular shopping and dining destinations, the desirable areas of Naples demand a higher price point, as do exclusive communities that boast a lot of high-end amenities. Neighborhoods west of U.S 41, also known as Tamiami Trail, are coveted because of the easy walking and biking distance to the beach.

Common sense tells us that prices tend to get more affordable as you get farther away from the beach. Yet here in Naples, that is not always the case. Residences within some of our gated communities, located east of Tamiami Trail, including Mediterra, Talis Park, Quail West, Collier's Reserve and Grey Oaks, can carry million-dollar price tags. Many attractive communities east of Interstate 75, including Heritage Bay, The Quarry, Riverstone and Saturnia Lakes, have single-family homes starting at $400,000.

New home construction has returned to Naples, as well.

Developers are bringing back to life communities that were deserted during the real-estate bust, with the goal of building them out, while others are clearing land and starting brand-new communities. Pulte, DiVosta, Centex, Stock and Del Webb are all back, along with some new builders, including FrontDoor Communities, to the Naples market. While this is encouraging, construction this time around is much more strategic. Builders are in direct competition with resales, which are also very affordable. With our market showing signs of improvement, builders are making their moves in a much more calculated fashion, so as not to produce too much inventory and overextend themselves.

Real Estate Services

A great place to start your real estate search online is www. NaplesArea.com, which provides a wealth of information.

It's the consumer home of The Naples Area Board of REALTORS® (NABOR) which is a local branch of the Florida Association of REALTORS® and the National Association of REALTORS®. NABOR has served the community for more than 60 years through its professionalism and adherence to a strict code of ethics. NABOR is the largest trade association in Collier County.

You can explore Naples communities, search both residential and commercial real estate, locate properties for sale and for rent--and even Find a Naples REALTOR to meet your needs.

Should You Rent or Buy?

If you'd prefer to rent in Naples as you ponder a home purchase, or even if you'd like to check out the options as you choose between renting and buying, plenty of help exists to help you find rental choices.

Searches on Craigslist.org and ApartmentGuide.com are two common websites on which to start your search for a Naples rental. Two other websites, AnnualRentals.com and NaplesRentals.com, focus solely on the Naples market. You might not think to enlist a Realtor in your rental search, but a Realtor can actually prove to be more helpful than perusing the newspaper classifieds. A Realtor who is knowledgeable about rentals will often know of units about to become available before they are announced to the general public. A Realtor will also be able to guide you in finding a suitable community that fits your needs. They've already done the legwork; they know what each community has to offer and which will be the best fit for you.

You can rent virtually anywhere and any style of home in Naples. While there are a few select apartment complexes in the area, many more private homeowners rent their homes, villas or condos out on a seasonal or an annual basis. Naples has lots of part-time residents and many are more than happy to rent out units that are not in use.

Rents vary based on location, home style, if units are furnished and unfurnished, and the time of the year. You may experience sticker shock with regard to rent prices, but deals can be found. Single-family homes and condos close to the beach command high rents for obvious reasons, but, beachside or not, rents will also be significantly higher if you plan to occupy a residence during Naples' high season, which is usually October through April. During the summer months, when our population drops considerably, rents are more affordable.

While seasonal rentals are popular here because we are a tourist destination, annual rentals are also prominent throughout the area. The primary difference between an annual rental and a seasonal rental is that annuals are usually unfurnished and the renter must be prepared to pay for lawn maintenance and utility and water bills during the term of the lease, while seasonal rentals are typically furnished and may not require the renter to pay out of pocket for services.

Unless you are in an apartment complex where the leases are in a standard format, leasing a private residence has many variables. Make sure you ask someone you trust to review a lease agreement between you and a homeowner so you know what to expect and what you are getting for your money.

When you are ready to buy in Naples, the easiest way to start your search is online at sites like Trulia, Zillow and Realtor.com to get a sense of prices and neighborhoods. You might also want to pick up one the local real estate publications, including *Homes & Land* and *Naples Homes*, or the *Naples Daily News*, whose Sunday edition includes a real-estate section.

Once you've narrowed down your choices, enlist the help of a Realtor who can guide you through the negotiations, the inspections, and all the steps leading up to closing.

CHAPTER 6

NAPLES IS A SHOPPING MECCA

Grocery and Gourmet Items

Foodies will enjoy food shopping in Naples, which boasts everything from big retail grocery chains to trendy organic shops.

Today, Publix grocery stores dominate the Naples landscape with what feels like a storefront on just about every corner in town. Publix offers a wide selection of food items, in addition to featuring bakeries, seafood and sushi counters, custom sandwich and rotisserie chicken departments, and an extensive wine and beer selection.

A tip about Publix: If a favorite product of yours is not stocked, ask an employee. Publix is happy to bring the product in for you. If it turns out to be a popular seller, it may just become part of its regular stock.

The oldest grocer in Naples, Wynn's Market, which opened in 1948, is still open today in a much larger location on Tamiami Trail, near downtown. Locals know and appreciate it for its gourmet items and butcher shop. The same can be said about Fresh Market, a lesser-known chain grocer located in the Park Shore Plaza, but one that is very popular with locals. Its specialty foods make it worth a visit.

A few Walmart Supercenters, as well as a Super Target, provide alternative options. A Walmart Neighborhood Market on Airport-Pulling Road is strictly a Walmart grocery, so you don't have all the other departments to distract you.

The trend toward healthy, organic and even gluten-free eating has found a following in Naples. Whole Foods and Trader Joe's recently entered the Naples market. Publix has developed a line of products called GreenWise, which have been incorporated within the regular stores. The positive reaction to GreenWise products prompted Publix to open two GreenWise markets in Naples to meet the needs of customers who prefer

natural and organic food choices. These stores are located at the Marketplace at Pelican Bay and at the Naples Plaza, across from Coastland Center.

A few independent stores, including Food & Thought, a grocery and a café off Tamiami Trail North; For Goodness Sake, in Berkshire Commons on Radio Road; and Earth Origins on Neapolitan Way, offer a mom-and-pop feel with shelves jam-packed with organic, vegetarian and vegan specialties.

Costco and Sam's Club are here, too, selling gourmet cheeses, baked goods, fruits and vegetables, and wine and liquor in bulk. Tip: Their oven-ready pizzas are a weeknight dinner pleaser.

Asian Pok Market and Asian Depot are ethnic food stores in Naples carrying a selection of Asian and Indian delicacies. Randy's Fish Market, Swan River and Captain Jerry's are known for fresh seafood, while Jimmy P's across from the Coastland Center is well-known for its meats and game.

Stock your wine refrigerator and liquor cabinet at Total Wine and ABC Fine Wine & Spirits, both of which are as big as a grocery store. The Wine Merchant, Decanted, Oakes Farm Market, World Market and Tony's Off Third offer more intimate settings for exploring fine wines and food pairings.

On weekends you'll find several farmers markets around town selling everything from fresh fruits and veggies to baked goods to home décor.

Source: Mike Dodge

Local folks selling the fruits of their labor can often be found off Third Street South in downtown Naples behind Tommy Bahama's, in the Galleria Shoppes at Vanderbilt, at the Collier County Government Complex off East Tamiami Trail, at St. Paul's Episcopal Church off Davis Boulevard, and in the parking lot of the Bed, Bath & Beyond plaza at the corner of Pine Ridge and Airport-Pulling roads.

Tip: If you are a master canner of foods and prefer to buy fruits and vegetables in bulk, take a drive out to Immokalee to the produce center off New Market Road, where you can buy tomatoes, corn, peppers, and more, by the case.

All-Inclusive Shopping Centers

Naples is also home to a few select, all-inclusive shopping and dining destinations: Waterside Shops, Mercato, Village on Venetian Bay, Tin City, Fifth Avenue South and Third Street South, and Coastland Center.

Waterside Shops

Source: Mike Dodge

Waterside Shops, at the corner of Pine Ridge Road and Tamiami Trail North, features more than 60 stores and restaurants. Anchored by Nordstrom and Saks Fifth Avenue, this high-end center boasts superior stores like Cartier, Ralph Lauren, Louis Vuitton, Kate Spade, Tiffany & Co. and Tory Burch. This is a place where you can enjoy complimentary valet parking and the assistance of a personal shopper. It's also home to Naples' only Apple store. Dining options include BrickTop's, Brio and California Pizza Kitchen.

Mercato

A few miles north, also off Tamiami Trail, is Naples' newest shopping and dining establishment, Mercato. Anchored by Whole Foods and Silverspot Cinema, Mercato is popular with the young professionals of Naples who enjoy its variety of shops, including Simply Natural, Bobby Chan, Charming Charlie, Coldwater Creek and Jos. A. Bank Clothiers. Places like Blue Martini, The Wine Loft and Burn by Rocky Patel come to life at night, giving Naples' singles places to relax with a cocktail and meet new people. Restaurants here are just as varied, from the reputable McCormick & Schmick's, The Capital Grille and Chipotle Mexican Grill to lesser-known, but equally delicious, AZN Azian Cuizine, Bravo! Cucina Italiana and The Pub Naples. If you want to live where you shop, Mercato has luxury residences above its storefronts.

Village on Venetian Bay

Wave to boaters while you shop at Village on Venetian Bay. This quaint shopping center, situated across the street from the Naples beach and along the bank of the Venetian Bay, has a variety of shops and restaurants, most of which are boutiques bearing names you may not recognize, but selling designer goods you will adore, including Charivari, Panache, J. McLaughlin and H.T. Chittum & Co. While perusing its singular stores, you can take a break at Ben & Jerry's for an ice cream or enjoy a meal of casual pub fare at The Village Pub. Come evening, bring the entire family back for dinner at Bayside, Cloyde's Steak and Lobster, M Waterfront Grille or Miramare.

Source: Mike Dodge

Tin City

Step back into Naples' history with a visit to Tin City, a grouping of tin-roofed buildings established in the 1920s. Today, Tin City is an indoor shopping haven whose more than 30 stores give you a great place to find a Florida souvenir to send back home to family, try Florida-made wines, purchase Naples-made soaps, and devour giant chocolate chip cookies. As a bonus, you can have lunch along the Gordon River.

Source: Mike Dodge

Fifth Avenue and Third Street South

Source: Scott Kelsey

Fifth Avenue and Third Street South in downtown Naples are popular destinations for visitors and residents alike. Locals appreciate the summer-long restaurant specials, which lure us downtown on weekend nights, and the eclectic shops, art galleries, and jewelry and clothing stores. With so many eateries to choose from, you can make a night of it by having appetizers at one, dinner at another, and dessert somewhere else.

Coastland Center

Coastland Center is Naples' traditional indoor mall. Anchored by JCPenney, Sears, Macy's and Dillard's, Coastland Center features more than 100 retail stores in addition to a food court and a children's play area. Some of the stores include Express, H&M, Hallmark, Kay Jewelers, Lady Foot Locker, Nine West, Victoria's Secret and Yankee Candle. Just like most malls across the U.S., this is where you bring the kids to have their photos taken with Santa at Christmas and where the teenagers shop with their friends on weekends.

A Few Miles Away

Outlet shopping exists at Miromar Outlets in Estero, just a few miles north of Naples. Gulf Coast Town Center in Fort Myers, just off Interstate 75 at Exit 123, is a showcase of more than 50 stores and more than 20 restaurants, and is home to Bass Pro Shops. And there's also Coconut Point Mall, off Tamiami Trail in Estero, which features more than 140 stores, including brand-name shops and big-box stores.

Strip Plazas

Nearly every corner in Naples has a strip plaza. Within those strip plazas are several stores, some independently owned and operated, others that are locally owned franchises, and still more that are well-known chains. Most are anchored by a Publix and/ or a drugstore like Walgreens or CVS. It's worth exploring to discover the stores you might be missing on your way to the big retail outfits.

Furniture and Design

You might find that the furnishings you bought for your previous home up north don't match your Florida surroundings. Not to worry. Naples has furniture retail stores in abundance. Well-known brands like Ethan Allen, Thomasville, Baer's and Havertys have their own showrooms. City Furniture, Ashley Furniture, and Rooms to Go all have immense stores around town. While each of these offer design services,  high-end furnishings and interior design specialists are found at boutique stores like Clive Daniel Home and Arhaus. If you want to go to a furniture design hub, the all-encompassing Miromar Design Center exists a few miles north in Estero. Within this massive building is everything you could possibly want to create the furniture of your dreams.

With so many people regularly moving to and from the area, our resale and consignment shops are always jam-packed. Many of the resale shops are affiliated with a charity, like the Shelter for Abused Women and Children, the Conservancy of Southwest Florida, St. Matthew's House and St. Vincent de Paul, so, your purchase will help someone in need while improving the look of your home.

A cluster of resale shops – Audrey's Attic, Bargain Box and Another Man's Treasures – can be found downtown along 9th and 10th Street North, with a few tucked along the adjacent avenues, including Options Thrift Shoppe and Ageless Treasures. Here you'll also find some auction houses and antique stores, which offer the occasional neat find. Others, like Healing Hearts and Habitat Home Store, are located along Tamiami Trail North and East, with a few individual shops situated along Naples' other main corridors.

If you are a pro at garage sales, you're in luck. Our year-around beautiful weather means it's always garage-sale season in Naples. Estate sales are also commonplace here. Sales by Sandy is a well-known source of quality merchandise, but you must be on an email list to find out about Sandy's future sale dates. To sign up, visit http://salesbysandy.home.comcast.net. You can also scour the *Naples Daily News* and Craigslist.org for locations and times. Who knows what bargains you'll find?

Dressing for Florida Life

Naples is a shopping haven. You'll probably find most of the stores you loved back home right here in Naples. We have stores for every style, from vintage to modern, and for every size budget.

Dressing to Beat the Heat

Having moved from the UK to Naples some five years ago, I understand the wardrobe challenges involved when transitioning from a four-seasons-a-year climate to one of year-round sunshine and warmth.

For starters, (although some residents still shudder at the thought) here in Southwest Florida, we can dispense with the rule against wearing white after Labor Day. We can have some pretty hot weather in September and white attire is a great way to beat the heat. If you still struggle with the idea of white, put away your lightweight, breezy whites and wear the hue in a heavier weight (white jeans, for example) or simply switch to a winter white or ivory; that way you'll enjoy the heat-busting benefits of white while feeling suitably seasonal.

Natural fabrics that breathe, such as cotton, linen, silk and bamboo, are your best friends in high heat. Sportswear fabrics with high performance wicking technology can be found in polo shirts and active wear; they're a must for the golf course or other outside activities. Sunblock is essential, and so too is a hat and sunglasses for protection against the fierce sun of high summer.

Source: Cheryl Lampard

Layering is a great way to dress in Naples. From October through until March or April, we can have some fresh mornings and cool evenings. Lightweight sweaters, wraps or jackets that can be added or peeled off as the day progresses are a must. Remember, too, that some restaurants and inside venues have the air conditioning ramped up so high that you'll need something to throw on to avoid a frozen shoulder.

Image Consultant and Style Maven Cheryl Lampard gained her love of fashion, eye for color and knowledge of the garment cut during her 20 years with some of the world's leading multi-national corporations, as well as her tenure running her own fashion, textile and retail business.

Department Stores

All the major retailers, including Kohl's, Dillard's, Nordstrom, Macy's, Bealls, JCPenney, have locations in Naples. Dillard's, Macy's, JCPenney and Sears are all located within Coastland Center, while Kohl's has a stand-alone store situated off Naples Boulevard. When Nordstrom announced it was coming to Waterside Shops in Naples a few years back, I believe you could hear the squeal of delight from women throughout Naples. Now, Nordstrom Rack, which carries merchandise from Nordstrom stores and Nordstrom.com at 50 to 60 percent off original prices, is coming to Mercato. Bealls, pronounced "bells," has several locations around Naples, including a couple of outlet stores where you can find discounted goods. You can spend your weekend afternoons perusing their racks or browse the aisles at Marshalls and Ross, which also have locations in town.

Target and Walmart have several superstores in Naples, to add to your shopping choices.

The Fashion Set

Naples has a very active social crowd that attends charitable events, with dinners running upwards of $500 a plate. To find the perfect party attire for such an affair, check out any of the fashion boutiques that line Fifth Avenue South and Third Street South in downtown, as well as Village on Venetian Bay and Waterside Shops, which offer unique, sometimes one-off creations. Some stores have a guard at the door and display no price tags. The old adage, "if you have to ask, you can't afford it," comes into play here. Cartier and Tiffany's at Waterside Shops help the high-end partygoers finish their ensembles with sparkling jewels.

Summer and Winter Attire

Given our year-round warm temperatures, many stores, including Chico's and Tommy Bahama, keep a wide selection of summer clothing available. The larger chain stores do change out their selections with the seasons, so when we experience the occasional cooler mornings and evenings, you can invest in a light sweater and closed-toe shoes.

Budget Shopping

For the more budget-conscious, our Goodwill and Salvation Army stores are huge and full of gently used clothing, thanks to the generosity of those who regularly pare down their closets. If vintage is your preference, try Audrey's Attic or Treasure Island.

For the Little Ones

Children's clothing boutiques in Naples include Lu Lu Belle, Twinkle Twinkle Little Store, Cottontails and Giggle Moon. Those looking for national chains will find Abercrombie Kids, Gymboree and Gap Kids.

Teenagers and young adults will probably prefer the shops at our only enclosed mall, the Coastland Center, where they will find Old Navy, American Eagle Outfitters and Forever 21.

Menswear

Guys will find a plethora of clothing choices at the well-known department stores. For those who want to show off their newfound Florida lifestyle, Tommy Bahama and Bealls offer that tropical look. When dressing up for a special occasion or a job interview, Men's Wearhouse and JoS. A. Banks cater to you. Then there are select stand-alone operations, like Mondo Uomo, Brooks Brothers, Teruzzi and Manny's Fine Menswear, that provide that one-of-a-kind look.

CHAPTER 7

NEVER A SHORTAGE OF THINGS TO DO

You'll find plenty of fun activities in Naples. Indoors or out, day or night, summer or winter, your event calendar is sure to be full.

Arts, Culture and Music

Bringing the world of art and entertainment to Naples has been a passion of many Neapolitans since the town's early days. In fact, the Naples Art Association was founded by three local artists in 1954. Decades later, Myra Janco Daniels, a lady whose name would become synonymous with the arts, put Naples on the map with the founding of the Philharmonic Center Cultural Complex in North Naples, which includes the Philharmonic Center for the Arts (now knows as Artis—

Source: Karen Plunkett

Naples), the Naples Museum of Art and the Naples Philharmonic Orchestra, whose former conductor, Keith Lockhart, now conducts the Boston Pops.

Source: Karen Plunkett

Today, because of these efforts, Naples is a cultural hub in Southwest Florida.

Big names, like Natalie Cole, Sheryl Crow, Jackie Evancho and Dionne Warwick, and Broadway shows, like "Billy Elliott," "Anything Goes" and even operas such as "Tosca," The Miami City Ballet, and the Philadelphia Orchestra also perform at the Phil. Even Alice Cooper has graced the Phil's stage! The Phil (now Artis) and the museum have an extensive calendar of events every season with something for everyone.

On 5th Avenue, the beautiful Sugden Theater is home to the Naples Players, whose roots date to 1952. Today, they deliver more than 200 theatrical performances annually.

In Old Naples, you'll find the von Liebig Art Center, a community arts center located at Cambier Park that offers changing exhibitions that are free to the public year-round. The center also has a full education program that teaches everything from photography to oil painting to those eager to hone their creative talents.

Source: Mike Dodge

A huge state-of-the-art band shell also nestles on this public parkland and is home to all sorts of performances. Just bring your lawn chair and enjoy the show.

If you enjoy the occasional outdoor concert, you'll love Summer Jazz on the Gulf, a free concert series hosted at the Naples Beach Hotel every year. The hotel's big expanse of lawn just steps from the Gulf of Mexico lets you relax with friends, savor the sunset, and appreciate musical performances by a variety of talented bands.

For those who like to peruse the works of artists from near and far, Naples plays host to several juried art shows and national art festivals throughout the year. You can see the canopies going up in Cambier Park, along Fifth Avenue South, and in some of the larger shopping plazas around town as artists arrive to show and sell their creations.

Source: Mike Dodge

Just outside of Naples, about 20 minutes up Interstate 75 in Estero, is Germain Arena, a huge indoor entertainment venue with more than 7,000 seats. Here you can see some of entertainment's biggest stars, from Elton John and Brad Paisley to the Zac Brown Band and Josh Groban. Shows for the kids include Disney on Ice, the Harlem Globetrotters, and the Ringling Bros. Circus.

Gastronomic Delights

Dining in Naples is as diverse as the nationalities of its visitors. Restaurants abound, offering everything from steaks and spaghetti to Thai and Tandoori and more. You'll find dining venues to suit every taste and every budget. With more than 400 restaurants throughout the area, you could dine at a different one every night of the year and still not hit them all. Enjoy dinner and a sunset view at a beachside restaurant – like the Turtle Club or HB's on the Gulf – one night, live music and homemade delicacies at a boisterous bar and grill – like Blue Monkey, McCabe's Irish Pub or The Real McCaw – the next.

Seafood is a local favorite and many establishments offer an extensive menu. Real Seafood Company, Truluck's and Nemo's are just a few of the fine dining restaurants known for their seafood selection; Riverwalk, Grouper & Chips and Pincher's Crab Shack are some that cater to the shorts-and-flip-flops crowd.

Source: Mike Dodge

Favorite Naples Dining Spots

Naples foodie Ivan Seligman regularly divulges his favorites on his blog, An Insatiable Appetite, and within the pages of *Gulfshore Life Magazine*. Here are the places he says are must-visits in Naples:

The Capital Grille
Fleming's Prime Steakhouse & Wine Bar
Preston's Steak House
USS Nemo
Fish
Café Normandie
Bha Bha Persian Bistro
Veranda E at Hotel Escalante
Manguro Japanese Sushi and Steak House
Cloyde's Steak & Lobster House
Café Alfredo
Sophia's
Bleu Provence
Charlie Chiang's
Inca's Kitchen
Aqua
Masa
Flaco's
Mr. Tequila's

We're known for our grouper and stone crab claws. Stone crab claws are a Florida delicacy enjoyed October 15 to May 15, with many Naples restaurants offering them on their menus. We even have a festival dedicated to the shellfish.

Naples boasts dishes from dozens of global cultures, as well as American dishes specific to their city of origin. Chicago deep-dish pizza and hot dogs, New York-style pizza, Kansas City ribs, and Chili 5 Ways from Cincinnati have also found a home in Naples.

Source: Gareth Rockliffe

Chain restaurants are here in abundance, too. In every strip plaza and mall and along every major roadway, good food is waiting to be found. If you have special dietary needs, gluten-free options are now on many Naples menus, and we are now home to our first vegan establishment.

Source: Scott Kelsey

Night Life

Late Night in Naples

There's nothing seedy about Naples nightlife.

Between the über-glitz of South Beach and the laid-back style of Tampa, Naples has carved out a late-night scene that is all about class. On Fifth Avenue, a champagne and caviar bar serves $900 bottles of Cristal and $1,000 plates of Ossetra. The place is Euro-sleek, done in white leather and glass accents, and after the dinner crowd has dispersed, the lights go down and a deejay sets up. He pumps techno and house music while the median age on the dance floor heads toward 25. This is Naples at its most haute.

Source: Artis Henderson

Down the street, a pub caters to the Sweet Caroline set, with live music and a slightly older crowd. The scene still isn't gritty -- we're still in Collier County -- but the vibe is more relaxed, more microbrew than Veuve Clicquot.

Less than 10 miles north, at the Mercato, at the collection of upscale shops and restaurants that has become the Naples after-dark destination, the ambiance is still classy even though we are, in essence, in a shopping mall. The crowd runs older earlier in the night, but as the sun sets and the dinner hours pass, the average age at the bars and lounges drops. By 11 p.m. there's a sea change: not a gray hair in sight. At the nightclub, the speakers crank, the disco ball whirls, and the space that had recently been filled with hurrying waiters is overrun with dancing bodies. Well-dressed dancing bodies. The sign out front says, "Fashionable attire required," and they're not joking. We may be throwing-distance from the county line, but this is still Naples.

Want Jell-O shots at 2 a.m.? You'll have to head north for that, to Fort Myers or Fort Myers Beach, where the crowd is more diverse and the dress code runs to tube tops and cut-offs. You might even find a mechanical bull. But if you want an upscale night out, where thousand-dollar caviar is a real option, Naples is a sure bet.

Artis Henderson has spent more than a decade exploring the hotspots of Southwest Florida. She writes the "Sandy Days, Salty Nights" column for Florida Weekly, where she chronicles her adventures along the Gulf coast.

Naples' sidewalks were known to roll up early in the past, but in recent years, as a younger demographic has moved in, nightlife has picked up. But only somewhat. Standalone nightclubs and Naples don't mix. Most that have opened over the years have just as quickly closed their doors, but a few survive. Vision Nightclub on Tamiami Trail North in Naples, Dimension Nightclub on Tamiami Trail East, Seven Nightclub in the Promenade at Bonita Springs are places where you can dance the night away. Naples is not South Beach by any stretch of the imagination, but we have some lively spots just the same.

Nightlife here is more about food, music and good times with friends. The three hotspots in town are Fifth Avenue South, Third Street South and Mercato.

Mercato, the newest shopping and dining destination in Naples, is hopping most nights. Guys like to unwind at Burn with a cigar, while the girls like to have cocktails at Blue Martini. Wine enthusiasts appreciate the new Wine Loft, which features jazz musicians.

Down on Fifth Avenue South, the atmosphere is more leisurely until later in the evening when a younger crowd comes in to enjoy the music at McCabe's and Yabba's.

A new free shuttle service, the Jump On Express, JOE for short, allows you to hop among Naples' three hotspots. It saves you cab fare, and you don't have to worry about traffic as you jump between Old Naples and North Naples.

Karaoke fans will find places around Naples to fulfill their need to belt out a few tunes, like South Street, Blue Monkey, The Quality Inn Tiki Bar, and Taste of Chicago. Live bands also grace the Naples night scene at various restaurants.

For something different, east of town is the Seminole Casino Immokalee, a large facility whose more than 1,200 slot machines and 34 live table games are open 24 hours, seven days a week.

Sports and Fitness

If you play a sport, you're sure to find a group here that shares your passion. You and a bunch of friends can enjoy a pick-up game of beach volleyball down by the Naples Pier. If you prefer a more organized event, bicycling enthusiasts here gather on early mornings, runners regularly participate in area marathons, and martial arts buffs train and compete at every level.

Golf

Golf is Naples' most popular sport. Given our reputation for having the most golf holes per capita, it's easy to see why. Golf courses here are designed by some of the greats: Jack Nicklaus, Arnold Palmer, Arthur Hills, Robert Trent Jones, Sr., and more. Our courses cater to every skill level. Naples has more private golf courses than public ones, but during the summer months many clubs participate in a reciprocal program that gives golfers the opportunity to play other courses around town that normally wouldn't be accessible by anyone other than members.

Some of Naples' public courses include Arrowhead, Eagle Lakes, Hibiscus, Ironwood, Naples Beach Hotel and Golf Club and Quality Inn and Suites.

Naples also hosts major golf tournaments throughout the year, from the Shark Shootout to the ACE Group Classic, bringing big-name celebrity golfers to the area to show off their talents.

Tennis

Tennis also attracts hundreds of local players. League tennis at area parks and clubs is a huge draw for many, offering play for all levels, as well as competitive events. The Collier County Community Tennis Association, the Col-Lee Tennis League and the Naples Inter-Club Tennis Association are a few worth contacting. Many communities, like Pelican Bay and Pelican Marsh, have huge tennis facilities and competitive programs that residents enjoy. Even smaller communities usually have at least a tennis court or two where you can perfect your serve.

Naples Parks

Collier County has a great public park system. At Golden Gate Community Center, Max Hasse Jr. Community Park, Veterans

Community Park, East Naples Community Park and North Collier Regional Park, racquetball, tennis and basketball courts, baseball and soccer fields, children's play areas, huge lap pools, walking trails and fitness centers are available to Naples residents and visitors.

Source: Collier County Parks and Recreation

North Collier Regional, off Livingston Road, is the newest addition to our park system. Its state-of-the-art facility boasts numerous sports fields, a large fitness room, and a fun-filled water park called Sun-N-Fun Lagoon.

Spring Training

Baseball fans can watch a live game just 30 minutes away. Spring training is huge in Florida, and the Boston Red Sox and the Minnesota Twins come to train in our part of the state. Hammond Stadium in Fort Myers is home to the Twins, while JetBlue Park, a brand-new stadium in Fort Myers, is the new training facility for the Red Sox. After the Major League leaves, the Fort Myers Miracle, a High-A Advanced Florida State League team, takes over Hammond Stadium for the season.

Ice Hockey/Ice Skating

You don't have to leave winter sports behind just because you've moved south. Ice hockey fanatics get their fill at Germain Arena in Estero, where the Florida Everblades play. Young ones can learn the sport through a variety of classes and eventually put their talents to the test as part of the youth hockey league. There's also an amateur adult hockey league with more than 40 teams. Your family can enjoy a day of ice skating at one of the two indoor ice skating rinks that are part of the arena. If you don't know how to skate, lessons are available, too.

Fitness

Fitness is important in Naples. Running, bicycling, mixed martial arts, yoga, CrossFit and more are all available to those who are focused on health and want to keep their summer beach bodies year-round. Packs of bicyclists in colorful attire are on the roads early in the morning, while fitness fanatics gather at area parks before the sun rises, participating in a rigorous boot camp.

Gulf Coast Runners, considered *the* running club of Southwest Florida, invites area athletes to its many social activities and races, while the Naples Velo Community, a growing group of cyclists, posts a full calendar of rides that are open to all.

5K and 10K runs are hosted regularly around town, most to benefit charities, in addition to fitness challenges and fun walks. Mud Runs and Color Runs, events that are growing in popularity around the country, have also come to Southwest Florida. If you're not familiar, Mud Run is a three- to five-mile course designed by firefighters, law-enforcement officers and members of the U.S. Special Ops teams, that takes participants through obstacles and mud on their way to the finish line, while Color Run is a two-mile course that splatters the runners/ walkers in bright colors.

Because our weather is awesome most days, many traditional fitness classes are held outdoors. You'll find Tai Chi on the beach and yoga on a paddleboard in the Gulf of Mexico. If you prefer to stick to the indoor gym, Naples has plenty, from intimate fitness rooms in your community clubhouse to large, state-of-the-art centers featuring pools, saunas and more. The personal trainers in town are on hand to take your workout to the next level.

Fresh Air: Exploring, Hiking, Kayaking, Fishing, Boating

With so many sunny days, it's no wonder people want to spend time enjoying the outdoors. A day at the beach is an obvious choice, but there are a ton of other things to do outside, too.

Boating

Boating is a huge activity in Naples. Many people own boats that are either housed at one of the local marinas or kept at a boat dock in the backyards, while others join boating clubs that offer fractional ownership. Still others simply enjoy the occasional boat rental. Boat ramps around town allow you to launch your vessel for $3 per day. Annual permits can be had for $120. Bayview Park, Cocohatchee River Park, Naples Landing and Collier Boulevard Boating Park are just a few of the boat ramps around town.

Local Attractions

Among our many popular destinations is the Naples Zoo, occupying acres of tropical gardens, where you can feed giraffes, watch primates swing from the trees, witness alligators swimming in the ponds, and, of course, view lions, tigers and bears. Quick tip: Collier County residents are admitted to the zoo free of charge on the first Saturday of every month. All you have to do is show your proof of residency.

Naples Botanical Garden is another favorite outdoor locale where you can stroll along miles of trails and view the beauty of a variety of cultivated gardens. The kids will adore the children's garden, where they can run through the water fountains, dig in the sand, and run through the fort. Purchase a membership and enjoy this oasis as often as you'd like. The garden offers plenty of places where you can curl up with a book or just relax in one the hammocks.

Source: Mike Dodge

The Conservancy of Southwest Florida is a great place to kayak, walk trails, and visit the wildlife rehabilitation center. Situated along the Gordon River, this facility offers electric boat cruises in addition to guided kayak tours, where you can learn about our native plants, birds and other creatures.

Fishing Charters and Sunset Cruises

Boating activities aren't limited to the Gordon River. Fishing charters that explore the back bays and the Gulf of Mexico run every day and, depending on the size of your party, you can choose an operation based on the size of the boat and the waters it navigates.

Sunset cruises are a favorite with tourists, but who says residents can't enjoy a relaxing boat ride, too? Naples Princess is a luxury yacht that offers dinner as you take in the Naples sights, while Double Sunshine is an open-air, double-decker boat with beer, wine, and a narrated tour. And there's Sweet Liberty, a 53-foot catamaran that sails the Naples Bay on sunset excursions. All of these depart from the vicinity of Tin City.

Birding

Bird watchers adore Corkscrew Swamp Sanctuary, which encompasses 13,000 acres in the heart of the Corkscrew Watershed, just east of Naples. The boardwalk that winds through the sanctuary treats you to a view of Florida's natural habitat that includes the largest remaining virgin bald cypress forest in the world. The colonies of wood storks, great blue herons, limpkins and anhingas that nest here will amaze you.

More Outdoor Recreation a Short Drive Away

Heading south toward Marco Island is Rookery Bay Natural Estuarine Research Reserve. Nestled among the mangroves, this protected area offers tons of outdoor recreation activities from kayaking and canoeing to fishing and photography. There's also a two-story exhibit hall where you can learn about Florida's coastal habitats and unique plant and animal species.

Just 30 minutes east on Tamiami Trail is Everglades National Park. You'll find airboat rides, eco-tours, kayak adventures, hiking and bicycling out there, and you can hold a baby alligator. This is the place to experience Florida in its natural state!

CHAPTER 8

BRINGING UP BABY AND BEYOND: DAY CARE, SCHOOLS AND ACTIVITIES

Whether you are moving here with children or plan to have a family some day, day care, schools and activities are going to play an important part in your relocation.

Infant and Toddler Care

Day Care choices abound in Naples. You can find everything from independently-operated facilities to church-affiliated programs and even hospital-based services. For a new parent, the choices can be overwhelming. While you might be tempted to research each school, simply Googling "day care in Naples Florida" generates more than 1.8 million results. Therefore, it might be best to ask friends and family for recommendations near your home or office.

A nanny may seem like an appealing option, and does work for some, but it can be costly. Searching a national website like www.care.com can help you locate a qualified nanny in Naples. While certainly not inexpensive, day-care centers are a more affordable option, usually running anywhere between $500 and $1,000-plus a month. The most popular day-care centers often have waiting lists, so contacting those centers sooner than later is a must. The age at which your child is entering day care or

95

school will have a big impact on your decision. If you are a working parent, your search may include a school that takes children who are merely weeks old. So Big So Bright Preschool, Naples Preschool Academy and Grace Community School are just a few that take infants. Even the Naples YMCA will take children as young as three months.

A host of churches provide infant and toddler care, including First Baptist Church, the Village School, Moorings Presbyterian, Our Savior Lutheran, and First Presbyterian, just to name a few. Church programs, especially for those who are members of that particular church, are attractive because the church may subsidize part of the cost.

For low- to middle-income families, the state of Florida also offers a voucher program, which helps alleviate some of the costs for families. To find out more, visit www.fundeducationnow. org.

Naples Community Hospital also offers an infant day-care center called Bear's Den Preschool. Hospital employees receive a discounted rate, and a limited number of spots are open to children of non-employees.

As your child nears school age, the Collier County Public Schools offer a comprehensive Pre-K program. Four year olds are eligible for Pre-K. For more information, visit www.collier.k12.fl.us/vpk. Children with special needs or disabilities are eligible for the Collier County Public School's Head Start program, which also takes children at age four. For more information, visit www.collier.k12.fl.us/headstart.

Public and Private Schools

If you have children, you'll be pleased to learn that Naples schools, both public and private, are highly ranked.

The Collier County public school system has a total of 48 schools serving a total student population of just over 44,000. The district includes 29 elementary schools, 10 middle schools and eight high schools. Roughly 3,200 teachers teach within the public school system.

Elementary Schools	2011	2012
Avalon	C	C
Big Cypress	A	A
Calusa Park	B	A
Corkscrew	B	B
Eden Park	C	D
Estates	B	A
Golden Gate	D	C
Golden Terrace	D	C
Highlands	C	C
Lake Park	B	A
Lake Trafford	D	D
Laurel Oak	A	A
Lely	C	A
Manatee	C	A
Mike Davis	A	A
Naples Park	A	A
Osceola	B	A
Palmetto	B	A
Parkside	D	D
Pelican Marsh	A	A
Pinecrest	D	C
Poinciana	B	A
Sabal Palm	C	C
Sea Gate	A	A
Shadowlawn	B	B
Tommie Barfield	A	A
Veterans Memorial	A	A
Village Oaks	C	C
Vineyards	A	A

Middle Schools	2011	2012
Corkscrew	A	A
Cypress Palm	B	B
East Naples	A	A
Golden Gate	B	B
Gulfview	A	A
Immokalee	B	C
Manatee	B	C
North Naples	A	A
Oakridge	A	A
Pine Ridge	A	A

High Schools	2011	2012
Barron Collier	A	A
Everglades City	F	C
Golden Gate	C	C
Gulf Coast	B	A
Immokalee	C	C
Lely	B	A
Lorenzo Walker	C	A
Naples	B	B
Palmetto	B	B

The public schools have large student populations. Multiple kindergarten classes, sometimes five or more, are enrolled at a single school. The facilities themselves are quite impressive, some featuring grand, two-story brick facades and all have excellent technology within. In fact, the Collier school district has approximately 27,000 networked computers of which nearly 22,000 are accessible to students.

According to www.collierschools.com, the student population is roughly 40 percent white, 44 percent Hispanic, 12 percent black and 2 percent "other." The attendance rate during the 2010-2011 school year was 95.43 percent. Collier's graduation rate was 81.3 percent during that same school year, while its dropout rate was roughly 1.9 percent. The district's total budget for the 2011-2012 school year was just over $938 million, equating to roughly $7,000 per student.

In addition to our public schools, Naples has a sizeable selection of private schools. Seacrest Country Day School and Community School of Naples are two private, non-denominational schools that welcome students from pre-K all the way through high school. Both are fairly pricey, with tuition running between $15,000 and $24,000 per year. Payment plans are available, as is financial aid, but there is no denying that a private education comes at a cost.

What do you get for your money? Both schools have excellent reputations and academic programs and a relatively small enrollment, which appeals to some parents. For example Community School has a total enrollment of just over 700, while Seacrest has around 450. This tends to keep the teacher-student ratio small.

Several other private schools affiliated with a religious denomination operate in Naples:

- The Village School of Naples is located on the campus of the North Naples United Methodist Church and teaches students from infant through eighth grade.

- St. Ann School, affiliated with St. Ann Catholic Church, teaches elementary and middle school students.

- First Baptist Academy, teaching pre-K through high school, has a total student body of just over 500 students.

- Naples Christian Academy serves grades kindergarten through eighth grade.

- Royal Palm Academy teaches kindergarten through eighth grade.

- St. John Neumann Catholic High School is a liberal arts school that is proud to tout its average class size of 15 students and its 100 percent graduation rate.

Quite a bit of research and evaluation goes into determining what school is best for your child. It may come down to class size, academics, athletics, the faculty, and the overall atmosphere and ambience of the school itself. Shopping for a school is similar to shopping for a home. You'll know when it feels right.

A Night Off From the Kids

Every parent needs a break, even if it's just for dinner and a movie, but finding a babysitter who you feel comfortable leaving your child with is challenging. You can always visit national websites like www.care.com, which qualify their sitters through various background checks, but it's always best to start with recommendations from friends and family.

You can always also put the word out at the local high schools that you are in need of a babysitter. Also, local colleges often have boards where students looking for opportunities to babysit will post a flyer or you yourself may post that you are looking for a qualified babysitter.

The average going rate for a babysitter is $10 per hour. If you have more than one child, expect to pay more.

If you're really struggling to find a babysitter you trust, several area gyms, including the YMCA and My Gym, offer Parents' Night Out, which allows you to drop off the kids and go enjoy yourselves for the evening.

Fun Activities for Young Ones

Your kids will never be bored in Naples. So many after-school activities, programs and sports are available that the most difficult part is choosing what to do.

The Collier County Park system offers a huge catalog of fun, affordable programs. Every park offers something, either after the regular school day or during the mornings and afternoons for those that are homeschooled or not yet of school age. The parks are also convenient on those days when your child's school has an early-release day or no school, providing programs specifically on those days to accommodate your work schedule.

Source: Collier County Parks and Recreation

If your kids love the pool, check out Sun-N-Fun Lagoon or the Golden Gate Aquatic Facility which both offer pools and slides, not to mention one- and three-meter springboards at Golden Gate and a "lazy river" attraction at Sun-N-Fun. Annual memberships are available. Kids can learn to swim through personalized swimming instruction or group lessons. They can also join swim and dive teams.

For a different kind of water activity, your kids might enjoy learning to sail or water ski on Lake Avalon at Sugden Regional Park.

Source: Collier County Parks and Recreation

For a more daring adventure, your kids might prefer BMX racing and freestyling, skateboarding or in-line skating at Fleischmann Park.

Through Collier County Parks and Recreation, your kids can learn everything from martial arts and fishing to junior-leader training and dance. There are also cooking classes and music lessons available, plus art of every medium.

And we haven't even touched upon team sports. Baseball, gymnastics, soccer, tennis, basketball, cheerleading and wrestling all have teams. Fencing, and even roller hockey, are options if your child is looking for a non-traditional activity. To view the entire catalog of the Collier County offerings, visit www.colliergov.net.

The YMCA in Naples also offers an array of activities, from swim lessons and dance classes to team sports, including soccer, T-ball, basketball, volleyball and cheerleading. The Y also recently introduced a new youth and teen wellness schedule open to young people from ages eight to 18 to help them develop healthy exercise and wellness habits. For more information on the YMCA programs, visit www.ymcapalms.org.

Source: Collier County Parks and Recreation

The Greater Naples Little League is yet another outlet for your kids. Each year, more than 360 boys and girls between the ages of five and fourteen take part in our national pastime. This is a volunteer organization, so your participation as a coach or a sponsor of your kids' teams is always welcome. Visit www.greaterNaplesLittleLeague.com.

If you've got a tumbler in your family, Naples has three great spots at which your child can hone those gymnastics skills. Naples Progressive Gymnastics, Gymnastic World Naples and Adrenaline Naples provide professional instruction and teach various techniques.

Source: Collier County Parks and Recreation

Within a 3,500-square-foot facility in Naples is House of Gaia, a community center offering a supportive learning and social environment for children, teens and families teaching them about multimedia art, culture, language, well-being, environmentalism, community building and volunteerism. For more information, visit http://houseofgaia.org.

Several places in town offer karate and various forms of martial arts, just as there are plenty of clubs that teach tennis, and still more places that teach art. If you've got a little actor in your midst, sign your child up for KidzAct, the youth theater troupe that performs at Sugden Community Theatre. Maybe you have a musician on your hands? If so, Kindermusik at Artis—Naples will help nurture their talent.

The Collier County Public Library also has a full calendar of free activities for kids and teens. Young children will enjoy story time, sing and learn, craft-making activities, and animal education events. Older kids will love learning astronomy, making tie-dye shirts, creating time capsules, and joining the young adult book club. Each branch of the library offers a packed schedule, so you'll never be at a loss for something to do. For the full schedule, visit http://public.collier-lib.org.

For a fun weekend family activity, visit the Golisano Children's Museum of Naples, a 30,000-square-foot facility off Livingston Road that combines fun with learning. The Museum also offers a variety of weeklong camps for children up to sixth grade, as well as homeschool programs. Visit www.cmon.org for more information.

Your children will have plenty to do for active fun in Naples. No matter what their interests, your kids will find a way to follow them.

College/Post-High School

Advanced Studies

Students have a rich array of higher-education options in Naples and Southwest Florida. Pursuits come in many different forms in Naples. For those who learn best in a traditional classroom setting, numerous brick-and-mortar establishments serve more than 45,000 local students. For those who like to set their own schedules, online courses are a convenient alternative.

Florida Gulf Coast University

In Naples' backyard is Florida Gulf Coast University (FGCU), whose campus encompasses 760 acres, 89 buildings and a 15-acre solar field. Its 450 faculty members teach 52 undergraduate degree programs, 30 graduate degree programs, one specialist program and two doctorate degree programs in its five colleges: Arts and Sciences, Business, Education, Health Professions and Public Services.

Source: Florida Gulf Coast University

Ranked by *U.S. News & World Report* as one of the top regional universities in the south, it's a big deal to have a school of this size just 20 minutes away. Founded in 1991, FGCU's student body has grown to nearly 13,000. A huge catalog of courses are available, from various kinds of engineering and all levels of education to journalism, marine science, music, political science and more.

The University is accredited by the Commission on Colleges of the Southern Association of Colleges and Schools. FGCU also offers a PGA Golf Management program and is one of just 20 colleges in the country accredited by the PGA.

Business Administration is one of the most popular majors on campus and FCGU's Lutgert College of Business has been recognized repeatedly by *The Princeton Review* as one of the best business schools in the nation. The Lutgert College of Business houses the Regional Economic Research Institute, the Small Business Development Center and the Lucas Institute for Real Estate Development and Finance.

Source: Florida Gulf Coast University

FGCU's civil, environmental and bioengineering programs have also been popular with the student body, leading to the establishment of the Whitaker College of Engineering, which now has its own dedicated building. In addition to academics, the university has a big athletics program, including golf, tennis, basketball, softball, baseball, cross country, volleyball, soccer, swimming and diving. Its teams compete at the NCAA Division I level. The FGCU men's basketball team recently put FGCU on the map when it became the first number 15 seed to reach the Sweet 16 in the NCAA tournament. Earning the name "Dunk City" during its historic run at the NCAA Division I title, the Eagles ignited national buzz and interest in FGCU that continues to this day.

Edison State College

Source: Edison State College

Situated on an 80-acre site off Collier Boulevard (also known as 951), Edison State College is the 13th-largest community college in Florida. It offers 10 Bachelor of Science and Bachelor's of Applied Science degree programs, including public safety administration, elementary education, nursing, supervision and management, secondary biology education, and more. The college also offers 18 associate in science degree programs, from architectural design and computer programming to dental hygiene and criminal justice; and associate in arts degree programs. More than 25,000 students attend Edison's four campuses, which are located in Lee, Collier, Charlotte, Hendry/ Glades counties as well as Edison online. While the majority of the students are 24 years old or younger, a large percentage, more than 40 percent, are over the age of 24.

Hodges University

Housed in two large buildings off Immokalee Road in Naples, Hodges University prides itself on turning out community and business leaders. Its accreditation by the Southern Association of Colleges and Schools enables it to award associate, bachelor and graduate degrees in all manner of subjects. The four schools under the Hodges umbrella speak to its line of programs: Johnson School of Business, School of Allied Health, Nichols School of Professional Studies and Fisher School of Technology.

Lorenzo Walker Institute of Technology

Founded in 1974, the Lorenzo Walker Institute, accredited by the Southern Association of Colleges and School, provides a workforce education and a job preparatory instruction. Some of its programs include automotive service technology, aviation maintenance technology, child care operations, cosmetology, drafting, nursing, massage therapy, surgical technology and legal administrative specialist. Approximately 600 students attend.

Wolford College

The newest addition to Naples' higher-education landscape is Wolford College, which moved into a permanent facility on Creekside Boulevard in June 2008. Wolford is an independent, single-purpose college with a 28-month curriculum that leads its students to a master's degree nurse anesthesia. It also offers a postmaster's doctor of nurse anesthesia degree, an online program for experienced CRNAs.

Ave Maria University

Located in the town of Ave Maria, just east of Naples, is Ave Maria University, a Catholic university whose liberal arts curriculum is supported by the teachings of the Catholic Church. On its

1,000 acres are a series of buildings designed in the tradition of Frank Lloyd Wright, including a library that houses 400,000 volumes and a field house that is home to its varied athletic programs. Ave Maria offers 21 majors and two pre-professional programs to its more than 800 students. The university is proud of its 15-to-1 student-faculty ratio and an average class size of 17.

Adult Education—Non-degree programs

Billing itself as a lifelong learning center, The Renaissance Academy of Florida Gulf Coast University, located on 5th Avenue South, focuses its efforts on adults, seniors and retirees who want to continue to learn without the high cost associated with higher education. The goal is to keep people learning and minds active through affordable, non-credit lectures, short courses, day trips, film series, writing workshops, travel abroad programs, day trips and more. There are no exams or grades, just learning. More than 10,000 Naples residents enjoy discussions on business and finance, computer instruction, interior design, philosophy, literature, music, government, photography, science, world affairs and more.

Community Education Classes

The Collier County Public Schools offer a comprehensive adult and community education program. Open to any adult, a variety of classes are offered throughout the year and held at one of the area high schools, usually during the late afternoon and early evening hours. Classes are fun and casual, yet give adults a chance to learn new skills, new technologies, and even languages. If you've always wanted to learn Spanish, Russian, Italian, German or French, you can. If you want to learn how to write for fun or for profit, you can do that, too. Sewing, painting, pottery, photography classes and more are all offered.

For those who are technologically challenged, you can learn tips and tricks on using the iPhone, Droid or Kindle Fire. Physical activity is covered in classes on Pilates, Tai Chi, yoga, Zumba, and ballroom dancing.

Because you have just moved to the golf capital of the U.S., you might find a beginner's golf class useful. Nearly every computer program, from Excel to Dream Weaver, is taught, as well as how to invest in stocks, how to buy your first home, how to buy gems, and even how to prepare yourself to become a U.S. citizen. Courses range from $59-$99 and you can view the entire course calendar and register online at www.collieradulted.com.

Prefer to teach a course? Download a course proposal online and submit it for consideration.

Student Housing

Source: Florida Gulf Coast University

Florida Gulf Coast University is the only local campus that offers student housing. At FGCU, a wide variety of community living exists both on and off campus. Suite-style residence halls in South Village, apartments in North Lake Village, and an off-campus apartment complex West Lake Village instantly make you feel a part of campus life. In all, the university can house approximately 4,200 students. To accommodate its growing student body, a new dorm able to house 520 students will open in the fall of 2014.

FGCU has also created special-interest housing, composed of students who live together in a residence hall and share a common interest. Right now, the Honors Community is composed of academic high-achievers, the Leadership through Service Community is committed to service, and the Wellness Community is focused on health and well-being. Greek life is also prominent at FGCU, with chapters of many national fraternities and sororities on campus.

CHAPTER 9

ASSIMILATE:
ASSOCIATIONS AND SOCIAL TIES

Volunteering is a fulfilling way to get to know your new community.

Charity organizations are numerous here and volunteering your time to one or a few is easy to do. What's amazing about Naples is that you will have the privilege of working and socializing with some of the elite, from millionaires and billionaires to famous authors, actors, athletes and CEOs. People in Naples are extremely generous and, no matter what their financial situation, they find time to volunteer and help one another.

Source: Cyndee Woolley

Best of all, doing something good for Naples will help you feel part of the community.

Local magazines, like *Gulf Shore Life*, *Naples Illustrated* and *é Bella*, devote several pages each month to those who make a difference in our community, giving you insight into how you may participate. A calendar of events can be found in each of these publications, as well as in the *Naples Florida Weekly* and the *Naples Daily News* newspapers. Who knows? One day your smiling face could appear in one of the party pages.

Source: Gulfshore Life

In addition to reading the local publications, it is also helpful to watch the local news stations so that you can learn exactly what's happening in Naples and stay up to date on the latest topics so that you can contribute to conversations at social functions.

Volunteer opportunities abound throughout Naples:

- Collier County public libraries: You can help with everything from adult literacy to book repair

- Area hospitals: You can do everything from delivering books to patients to working in the gift shopNaples

- Botanical Garden: You can serve as a docent or get your hands dirty raking, weeding, potting and trimming

- Humane Society: Play with the cats, help train the dogs, or foster an animal in your home until it is ready for adoption

- Avow Hospice: Provide companionship to patients or assist with clerical duties

- Naples Zoo: Aid with animal diet preparation or support membership by helping with mailings

- Neighborhood Health Clinic: Assist in the café, wash lab coats and even pitch in at the pharmacy

- Shy Wolf Sanctuary: Raise funds, plan events and introduce the community to the facility

- Habitat for Humanity: Do your part in building a house, participate in selecting a family who will be the proud owners of that house, or work in the retail store

- St. Matthews House: Serve meals, organize the food pantries or assist in the kitchen

Visit www.volunteercollier.org, a site that matches volunteers with opportunities.

Joining a club or an organization is another great way to get involved and feel like part of Naples.

Naples offers a ton of organizations, associations and groups that get together on a regular basis for some combination of fun, charity work, and business. Naples is all about networking and finding the group that speaks to you.

Source: Community Foundation of Collier County

The *Naples Daily News* publishes a weekly list of clubs and organizations in its Sunday edition. You can also view the list online at http://www.Napleschamber.org. You'll be surprised to find a group for almost every interest.

There's a Naples Moms Society, Young Professionals of Naples, a Women's Network of Collier County, a Vegetarian Society, a Naples Jewish Social Club, a dog club, a Scrabble Association, a Quilters Guild, a Muscle Car Club, a walking club, a writer's association, and so much more.

Some folks have formed their own networking groups based on their nationalities, the colleges they attended, or the town they are from, just to meet like-minded people. On the off chance that you don't find what you're looking for, take a cue from these folks and start your own group.

Nearly everyone in Naples is from somewhere else, meaning they were once new, too. Sometimes the best place to start meeting people is within your own community. Many Naples communities offer a full social calendar giving you an opportunity to meet your neighbors. An evening social down at the clubhouse, an organized card game, a theme night dinner party in the dining room, or a community blood drive will have you meeting people in no time. Because nearly every community has a pool, you have a good chance of meeting someone while soaking up the sunshine.

Tip: Tell your neighbors you are new to the community and would love to meet them at a potluck or cocktail hour at your new house! Invite them via a mailed postcard or via email through your community website.

If you happen to live in a community with no organized social calendar or website, you can always meet people at your place of business, through your child's school, or through a group with a shared interest.

Local Media

Local news, traffic and weather are on:

- NBC-2
- ABC-7
- FOX 4
- Wink TV

Naples has 54 radio stations within listening range, but the local stations include:

- 89.5 FM Christian contemporary
- 90.1 FM Public radio
- 90.9 FM Religious
- 91.5 FM Religious
- 91.7 FM Public radio
- 92.5 FM News/Talk
- 94.5 FM Classic rock
- 95.3 FM Classic hits

- 96.1 FM Classic rock
- 96.9 FM Hot AC
- 98.9 FM Talk
- 100.5 FM Spanish
- 101.1 FM Easy listening
- 101.5 FM Religious
- 101.9 FM Country
- 103.9 FM Top 40
- 104.7 FM Hot AC
- 105.1 FM Religious
- 105.5 FM Hip Hop
- 106.3 FM Adult contemporary
- 1240 AM News/Talk
- 1270 AM News/Talk
- 1350 AM Sports
- 1410 AM Adult album alternative
- 1480 AM Adult album alternative
- 1660 AM Adult album alternative

Local newspapers include the *Naples Daily News* and the *Naples Florida Weekly.*

Local magazines:

- Gulfshore Life
- Naples Illustrated
- é Bella
- Pulse
- Fifth Ave
- Natural Awakenings
- Gulfshore Business
- Business Observer
- Fit Nation Magazine

CHAPTER 10

PRACTICAL NOTEBOOK ON MOVING

Moving Calendar

Second-home owners, seasonal tenants and snowbirds tend to move in during Naples' high season of November through April. Families living in Naples full-time generally move to another part of town during the summer months, when school is out.

Source: William C. Huff Companies

If you have a choice of when to move, consider the weather first. The summer months can be uncomfortably hot and humid and the afternoon rains can make moving even less enjoyable than normal. During the winter months, while the weather is much more favorable, increased traffic can make moving slow.

Keep this in mind when selecting your moving date: the first and last few days of the month tend to be the busiest moving times, so avoid them; and holiday schedules might result in unnecessary delays.

Moving Assistance

Downsizing to Fit the Florida Lifestyle

You may have fallen in love with Naples, but the idea of moving stirs up a flood of emotions, from excitement to anxiety. Up north you have attics, basements, garages and sheds. Here, storage within the home is limited.

The worst thing you can do is pay a moving company to ship all your items to Naples, only to find that no one wants the items after they have been moved. Our consignment shops and donation centers are full and unwanted belongings are turned away frequently because of this phenomenon.

Source: E. Sue Huff & Associates, Inc.

These tips will help you start sifting through your household collections and downsize to a more manageable Florida lifestyle:Use concentric circles. Assess your home and compartmentalize items. Start with the outermost part of your house, in place that are farthest from the everyday living spaces. Items in those parts of the house are likely to be things you don't use or need. That's why they are there, right? They are out of sight.

- Evaluate your collections. Most of us collect something, whether it's figurines, sports memorabilia, coins or vintage dinnerware. It can be difficult to part with these, but how important will these be in the twilight of your life? Find out if someone, an antique dealer or a collections memorabilia dealer, will take at least some of them or ask family members if anyone has had an eye on one of your collectibles.

- Sort through family pieces and the things the kids left behind when they moved out. These can be the hardest decisions, but, ultimately, if the kids are far away, or if they are too busy to let you know if they want it, there comes a point when you have to pull the trigger.

De-cluttering can be hard emotionally, but once you get through the decisions on what to keep and discard from the parts of your home that are generally unused, the living space is usually worth storing and shipping. Inside the house, start with the closets, under the sinks, and the pantry. The very last places to pack are those items on the walls, the dining and living rooms, and the master bedroom. Following this process makes the move easier.

Professional downsizing coach, Jim Henderson, president of William C. Huff Companies, a moving and storage firm with offices in Naples and Barrington, NH, specializes in moving households.

Moving to a new state from several states away can be a bit overwhelming and intimidating, but a moving consultant or a broker can assist you with all of the details. A personal relocation consultant will inquire about taxes, duties and restrictions involved with moving your items.

If you decide to go it alone, many of the large, professional moving companies, like North American Van Lines, United Van Lines and Apple Movers, offer online quotes and reviews of their services. A contingent of Naples moving companies partner with the national outfits to bring your belongings to Naples from another state. Some include:

- Ray the Mover
- William C. Huff Moving and Storage
- Peluso Movers
- Naples Moving and Storage
- All My Sons Moving & Storage
- Two Men and a Truck
- Best Moving & Storage

For a full-fledged, concierge-type move, visit www.movingforlove.com, a new website that specializes in helping people move to a place they have fallen in love with, all with the help of a personal assistant.

Additionally, consider what of your home's belongings you need to bring to Naples. Not everything that you own will be suitable in your new Florida home. For instance, cold-weather clothes can be sold or donated. In some cases, it may just be easier and more cost-efficient to sell your home furnished or sell the furnishings before you move and move to Naples with only your most intimate belongings.

Transport and Logistics

When moving from another state, you may think renting a truck is the best way to go, but it can be more costly than you think. Make sure you take into account the need for fuel and tolls. Sometimes hiring a company to drive your items down to Naples is more economical.

Freight shipping is a great way to ship vehicles, antiques, or even your whole house packed up in boxes. Big, bulky items are best shipped this way because it's easy and the most economical. Visit the www.freightcenter.com for more information.

Car carriers are another way to get your vehicle here. A big indicator that season has arrived in Naples is all the car carriers filled to capacity and often parked in front of a gated community, waiting to unload.

If you are renting a small place until you buy a larger home that will accommodate all of your household items, Naples has an incredible amount of storage places where you can safely store your items until you're ready for them.

Source: William C. Huff Companies

Prices vary by size of the unit, if the unit is air conditioned, and by length of the rental period.

Here are a few located around town:

- Naples Self Storage Units on Airport-Pulling Road
- Public Storage on Radio Road
- Naples Self Storage on Pine Ridge Road
- Olde Naples Self Storage South on Goodlette-Frank Road
- Guardian Personal Storage on David Boulevard
- Goodlette Self Storage on Goodlette-Frank Road
- The Lock Up Self Storage on Piper Boulevard
- Cypress Self Storage on Preserve Lane

An Overseas Move

Some tips for those moving to Naples from overseas:

- Moving by sea can be a long process, taking about six to eight weeks to get all of your household goods to your new Naples home.

- Moving by air is expensive, but is becomingly increasingly popular because it eliminates the expense of a long hotel stay while your possessions are en route.

- Typically, the belongings of a small family with an average living and dining room, two bedrooms, a kitchen and miscellaneous books, clothes, dishes and décor, would be enough to fill one standard 20-foot container whose 1,000 cubic feet can hold approximately 6,000 pounds of goods. Larger households may require a 40-foot container.

- Do not pack your own boxes when planning a long-distance move. Leave it to the professionals.

- Ensure that your international moving company is licensed with the Federal Maritime Commission as an Ocean Transportation Intermediary. A reputable mover will be licensed with a tariff and bond.

- Contact the U.S. Embassy to get advice on visas. Personnel may even be able to put you in contact with other expatriates who can share their experiences and provide you with valuable advice.

- Additional insurance is always advisable.

- If you are shipping your car or truck, expect plenty of restrictions, hefty costs, and consider whether or not you are licensed to drive in the U.S. upon your arrival, and if your vehicle meets the environmental standards.

- If you have pets, check on quarantine requirements.

(Sources: Mover Max, 123 Movers, International Sea & Air Shipping)

Upon the arrival of your household items in the U.S., most, if not all, will be subject to an X-ray procedure. Some containers are randomly selected for a physical inspection, which could result in a delay in customs clearance. Customs clearance will take on average between four and eight days from date of arrival. All non-U.S. citizens must be in the U.S. when the shipment arrives.

Import documentation is checked thoroughly. Make sure you have filled out the proper fields on U.S. Customs Form 3299. A Supplemental Declaration for unaccompanied personal and household effects and a Power of Attorney is also required if you cannot be present at customs for your shipment to clear. Also, a copy of your work visa and a copy of your passport are needed.

For more information, visit www.internationalmoving.com.

CHAPTER 11

THE ECONOMY

Source of Vitality

Tourism, by far, is one industry that drives the Naples' economy.

People vacation here from all over the world. From January through November 2012, more than 1.44 million people visited the area, according to the Naples, Marco Island, Everglades Convention and Visitors Bureau. This was nearly a six percent increase over the same time period in 2011.

Those visitors had a total economic impact of more than $1.3 billion, a more than 11 percent increase over 2011. To accommodate all of these visitors, area businesses that cater directly to leisure and hospitality employ roughly 22,000 in the off-season and nearly 26,000 during the peak season.

The Ritz-Carlton Naples and the Waldorf Astoria Naples are huge employers in the area, with approximately 1,000 employees each between the two resort properties.

Source: Cindy Dobyns

Two more industries that drive the Naples economy are real estate and construction. This is the land of vacation and second-home ownership, so it's easy to see why real estate is such a huge contributor; and it wasn't all that long ago that new homes couldn't be built fast enough to accommodate the insatiable buyer demand.

Naples has been growing at a quick clip. Take a look at our census numbers:

- 1980: 85,971

- 1990: 152,099

- 2000: 251,377

- 2010: 321,520

After the 2000 Census numbers came out, demographers predicted that the population of Naples would be well over 350,000 by 2010, and over 405,000 by 2015. However, while the growth rate has not been as strong because of the national economic troubles in recent years. In the early part of the decade, Naples was growing at a rate of five percent annually, but between April 2010 and July 2011, our growth was only 2.1 percent.

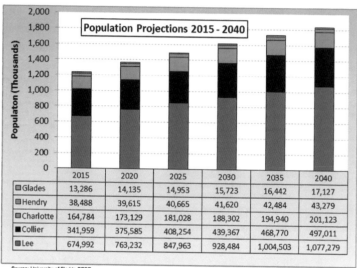

	2015	2020	2025	2030	2035	2040
Glades	13,286	14,135	14,953	15,723	16,442	17,127
Hendry	38,488	39,615	40,665	41,620	42,484	43,279
Charlotte	164,784	173,129	181,028	188,302	194,940	201,123
Collier	341,959	375,585	408,254	439,367	468,770	497,011
Lee	674,992	763,232	847,963	928,484	1,004,503	1,077,279

Source: University of Florida BEBR

Of course, construction dried up after the boom of the mid-2000s ended. Real estate prices and sales took a dive as a result. And Naples' population, which was rising steadily, decreased as jobs became scarce and homes were lost. Today, both of those industries have bounced back and recovered nicely.

- Buyers are back scooping up well-priced homes

- The inventory of existing homes for sale is down to historic lows

- Prices have stabilized and, in some pockets, are on the rise

New home construction has followed suit, with building permits on the rise, although still below their peak levels in 2005. In

Collier County, single-family home-building activity increased 55 percent in 2012, with 1,270 permits pulled, reported Randy Thibaut, of Land Solutions Inc., at the Market Watch 2013 event. Builders are more strategic in their new-home pursuits today than they were during the boom. Some of the larger, more notable builders, including Taylor Morrison, WCI, GL Homes, and Stock Development, have begun to build again in new and existing communities throughout the area. The increase in residential construction has brought subcontractors back to Naples, contributing to our job growth.

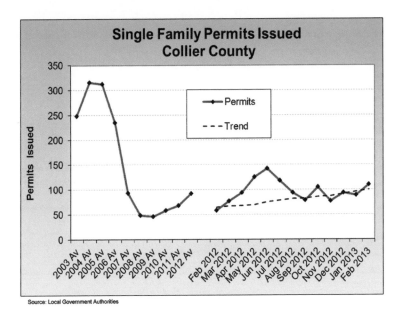

Source: Local Government Authorities

Despite the beating that the construction industry took in the last few years, a handful of developers and contractors, including WCI Communities, Manhattan Construction, DeAngelis Diamond, B&I Contractors, Owen-Ames-Kimball, Stevens Construction and J.L. Wallace, continue their legacy as top companies in our area based on revenue.

Other industries that significantly contribute to Collier County's economy are retail, finance, insurance and agriculture.

Efforts to Diversify the Economy

Since the most recent recession, efforts have been made to diversify the Naples economy to reduce reliance on real estate, construction and tourism, which took such a hard hit. Emerging industries now include computer software and services, distribution, and health and life services.

In order to send the message that "Collier County is open for business," the Greater Naples Chamber of Commerce created The Partnership for Collier's Future Economy to help support a business climate conducive to growth. Government officials are now reaching across county lines to partner with one another in this diversification effort. The goal is to bring more high-paying corporations and research facilities to the Southwest Florida region.

In recent months, banks, private equity and hedge fund firms are finding favorable business conditions in Florida. According to the Tax Foundation, Florida is the fifth-most-favorable state in the nation to do business. By comparison, New York is at the bottom, as the least favorable state. The recent moves by some businesses to Florida show the interest in taking advantage of the lack of a state income tax.

Efforts to diversify are taking root. Today, some of the top companies in our area, as reported by *Gulf Shore Business Magazine*, are now healthcare-related operations and tech firms.

Top Local Companies

Based on revenue, these are some of our area's top companies:

- Health Management Associates: With 71 acute-care hospitals in 15 states, including Physicians Regional Medical Group on Collier Boulevard and on Pine Ridge Road, HMA is a big employer in our area.

- Fifth Third Bank: A financial institution headquartered in Naples with nearly 700 employees spread out over more than 60 banking centers throughout seven counties.

- NCH Healthcare System: Includes the NCH Downtown Naples Hospital Campus and NCH North Naples Hospital Campus, and employs close to 4,000.

- Healthcare Network of Southwest Florida: With medical and dental service locations throughout Naples, this not-for-profit healthcare provider employs approximately 250.

- WCI Communities: Based in Bonita Springs, this developer/homebuilder with 700 employees is selling and building in nine area communities.

- INgage Networks: Headquartered in Naples, this inspired company uses innovative strategy and online software to help other companies maximize their customer, partner and employee relationships.

- Premier Sotheby's International Realty: With several offices up and down the Gulf Coast, this luxury real-estate brokerage firm employs about 450.

- Bob Dean Supply: A distributor of industrial power transmission, industrial supply and pump products.

- Merits Health Products: A home-medical equipment distributor.

- TIB Financial Corp.: With more than 1,350 employees, this financial services company, a subsidiary of Capital Bank Financial Corp., operates as the bank holding company for Capital Bank.

- Hope HealthCare Services: Employing nearly 1,100, this healthcare operation includes Hope Hospice, Hope Healing Hearts, Hope Kids Care and Hope Parkinson Program.

- Beasley Broadcast Group: Owns 44 radio stations throughout the U.S., including five here, with its corporate offices in Southwest Florida. Employs more than 400.

- Chico's FAS: This women's clothing retailer operates more than 1,200 stores in the U.S. and employs nearly 5,000.

Headquarters and Branches

Larger corporations are choosing to relocate their corporate headquarters or place a company branch in Naples and Southwest Florida.

Here is a sampling:

- NeoGenomics Laboratories, a publically traded company specializing in genetic testing for cancer, is headquartered in Fort Myers. It employs approximately 130 people locally and is currently undergoing a three-year expansion which is expected to create 75 new jobs.

- Arthrex, a privately-held medical-device company that develops new products in the field of orthopedics, is headquartered out of Naples. Its workforce of more than 800 is housed within several buildings off Creekside Boulevard, and the company has plans to expand its employee base and its facilities with the construction of a new building near Ave Maria.

- Gartner Inc., an information technology research and advisory company, has a branch in Fort Myers where it

132

employs approximately 350. It is expanding its facilities in Southwest Florida by 20,000 square feet.

- Source Interlink Companies, headquartered in Bonita Springs, is an integrated media, publishing, merchandising and logistics company.

- Chico's FAS dates back to 1983 as a small boutique store in Sanibel Island. Today, headquartered in Fort Myers, it encompasses Chico's, White House Black Market and Soma Intimates boutiques and outlets.

- Heinz North America has a manufacturing branch in Fort Myers that produces some of the company's frozen specialties and frozen pastries.

- Hertz Corporation is moving its world headquarters from New Jersey to a 34-acre parcel in Estero where a 300,000-square-foot facility with car rental and sales operations will house at least 700 employees.

- Structure Medical, headquartered in Naples, manufactures medical implant products used by orthopedic surgeons. Since opening in 2004, it has also opened a second facility in North Carolina.

- ASG Software Solutions has its worldwide headquarters here in Naples. Just as its name implies, it provides large businesses with software solutions.

Other major employers in our area include Publix, a grocery store with several locations throughout town, Walmart, which has three super centers in Naples alone, and First National Bank of the Gulf Coast, which is headquartered in Naples.

Why Companies Locate in Naples and Southwest Florida

A key factor in a company's choice of Southwest Florida as a business location is the quality of life, which attracts top talent. Southwest Florida also has strong incentive programs and a Foreign Trade Zone at the Southwest Florida International Airport.

Collier County also features one of the lowest ad valorem tax rates in Florida. The state corporate income tax is 5.5 percent and the sales tax is six percent. The county also offers two Enterprise Zones in Immokalee and Everglades City, which offer special tax incentives to businesses. Two venture capital firms call Collier County home: Gulf Coast Venture Forum and Tamiami Angel Fund.

Just to our north, Lee County's Office of Economic Development has two incentive programs in place: the Lee County Job Opportunity Program to leverage 80 percent state funds and 20 percent county funds based on the number of new jobs a company creates, and a set-aside fund for larger companies that create at least 75 new jobs.

The Collier County Government Center reports that, on a per capita basis, Collier County has more CEOs and more successful business experience than any other community in the United States. It also has the second-highest level of patent activity in Southwest Florida.

Entrepreneurial Pursuits

The vast majority of our local businesses are small- to medium-sized firms led by entrepreneurs. In fact, Naples and Southwest Florida abound with entrepreneurial success stories. For example:

- Norman Love, founder of Norman Love Confections, who started making handcrafted chocolates in his facility in Fort Myers in 2001 and is now known worldwide for his sweet treats.

- Naples Soap Company, which opened its first retail store in 2009 and now operates five retail locations across Southwest Florida, plus, an online store along with seven shops in Tokyo, Japan.

- Joanne Glasgow, of Simply Cupcakes of Naples, who was responsible for bringing the cupcake craze to Naples.

- Hong Long and Felix Lluberes, whose Naples-based business Position Logic made the 2012 Inc. 500 List of fastest-growing private companies in America.

- Benjamin Fleischer, of Pyure Brands in Naples, is changing the food and beverage industry with his Stevia product, an all-natural, zero-calorie sweetener.

- Michelle Spitzer, founder of Maid Pro, took a Hodges University class assignment and turned it into a multimillion-dollar business.

Entrepreneurs in Naples will find a ton of support. The Greater Naples Chamber of Commerce offers classes, resources, contacts and videos to help you start or grow a business, while the non-profit organization SCORE pairs you with an entrepreneurial mentor of similar background to guide you through all-things business. At Florida Gulf Coast University, the Small Business Development Center helps owners grow their businesses through a collection of programs and services.

You can join the Entrepreneur Society of Naples to meet fellow business owners or join VentureX, an innovative, 8,000-square-foot workspace at Mercato in North Naples that rents collaborative work areas and technology to independent professionals.

Local business publications, including *Gulfshore Business*, *Southwest Florida Business Today*, *Focus Magazine* and *Business Currents*, give insight into the area's trends, spotlight local up-and-coming companies, and offer tips for success.

Employment Market

Naples' largest public employers include the public-school system, the county government and the county sheriff's office.[1] In the private sector, NCH Healthcare System, Publix Supermarkets, Chico's and The Ritz-Carlton have a large employee base.

Here is a list of the largest employers in Collier County[2]:

Employer
NCH Healthcare System
Gargiulo Inc.
Collier County Sheriff's Office
Home Team Inspection Service
Publix Supermarkets
Marco Island Marriott Beach Resort
Waldorf Astoria
Bentley Village
Gulf Bay Group
Moorings Park
Ritz-Carlton
Walmart Supercenter
U.S. Postal Service

Naples' unemployment rate dropped considerably in 2012, from 9.3 percent in January to 7.8 percent by December. And yet, though companies are hiring, wages haven't bounced back as quickly. The state's minimum wage increased to $7.79 an hour in 2013, up from $7.67.

Here are the top 25 highest-paying jobs in Collier County[3]:

Occupation Title	2012 Annual Median Level Wage
Chief Executives	$169,906.63
Family and General Practitioners	$163,978.26
Dentists, General	$142,865.99
Pharmacists	$131,063.58
Computer and Information Systems Managers	$130,675.44
Engineering Managers	$118,305.65
Transportation, Storage, and Distribution Managers	$118,149.57
Sales Managers	$113,927.35
Financial Managers	$110,183.57
Human Resources Managers, All Other	$108,690.14
Marketing Managers	$103,359.07
Securities, Commodities, and Financial Services Sales Agents	$101,395.69
Civil Engineers	$97,024.71
Medical and Health Services Managers	$96,992.59
Veterinarians	$96,234.22
Natural Sciences Managers	$94,599.43
Industrial Production Managers	$93,051.93
Purchasing Managers	$92,919.31
Administrative Services Managers	$92,445.99
Managers, All Other	$92,270.53
Lawyers	$92,128.15

Occupation Title	2012 Annual Median Level Wage
First-Line Supervisors/Managers of Fire Fighting and Prevention Workers	$89,922.45
Architects, Except Landscape and Naval	$88,306.94
Physical Therapists	$88,181.81
General and Operations Managers	$88,085.04

Area companies with the highest number of job openings advertised online[3] include NCH Healthcare System, Marriott International, Arthrex and Health Management Associates. Industries with the highest job openings include health care, retail, hospitality, manufacturing, professional and technical services, arts and entertainment, finance and insurance, and real estate.

[1] www.FloridaTaxWatch.org *May 2012*

[2] *EmployFlorida.com 2012*

[3] *EmployFlorida.com as of February 27, 2013*

Economic Indicators

Real estate is a leading indicator of what is to come here in Southwest Florida. A recent increase in residential construction has spurred job growth. New developments are coming online regularly.

Plans for more retail establishments are also strong, and experts in the field believe that commercial construction will grow at a moderate rate in 2013. Trash collection is also an economic indicator. In a recent *Business Observer* article, Larry Berg, senior district manager for Waste Management in Naples, reported that residential bulk waste (sofas, refrigerators, appliances, etc.) rose nine percent for the first nine months of 2012, compared to the same period in 2011. This kind of trash means homeowners are renovating, a sign of improving consumer confidence and an increase in real estate transactions.

CONCLUSION

The pages of this book demonstrate that Naples is more than a beachside retreat for the wealthy, more than a winter getaway for those temporarily escaping the cold north, and much more than a retirement destination.

Young professionals are discovering that top companies in the medical and technology fields not only exist here, but are expanding their operations, too, providing jobs for eager college grads as well as experienced employees looking to boost their resumes.

Seasoned workers seeking a new challenge are finding a market open to new entrepreneurial pursuits. Growing families are finding affordable housing, excellent healthcare, and good schools. And active adults are finding plenty of activities and attractions to meet their busy lifestyles.

Most importantly, everyone is finding a quality of life here that many didn't believe they could actually enjoy until their golden years. The joy of life in Naples is waking every day to sunny skies and swaying palms. The drive into work or school is not hindered by traffic jams and long commutes. And at the end of the day, you can easily swing by the beach for a sunset stroll.

Why should retirees have all the fun? Naples offers so much for all ages.

You could be enjoying the Florida lifestyle now and reaping the benefits of no state income tax, lower property taxes and energy costs, and affordable housing.

Isn't it time you moved to Naples?

GO ONLINE FOR OUR EXTENSIVE LIST OF NAPLES RESOURCES

For the latest information about moving to and living in Naples, please visit our companion website:

http://www.MovingtoNaplesGuide.com.

If you need to access our extensive resource pages quickly, go directly to: http://www.MovingtoNaplesGuide.com/resources/

Important Phone Numbers and Website Links

City of Naples Government
(http://www.naplesgov.com)
(239) 213-1000

Collier County Property Appraiser
(http://www.collierappraiser.com)
(239) 252-8141

Drivers Licenses
(http://www.colliertax.com/driverslicense.html)
(239) 434-4600

Fishing Licenses
(http://www.colliertax.com/hf.html)
(239) 252-8176

Marriage Licenses
(http://www.collierclerk.com/recording/marriagelicenses)
(239) 252-7241

Social Security
(http://www.colliergov.net/index.aspx?page=1125)
(239) 530-3364

Tax Collector
(http://www.colliertax.com)
(239) 252-8171

Vehicle Registration
(http://www.colliertax.com/motorvehicle.html)
(239) 252-8177

Voter Registration
(http://www.colliervotes.com)
(239) 252-8450

Beach Parking Stickers

Naples City Hall
(http://www.naplesgov.com/index.aspx?NID=353)
(239) 213-1826

Collier County Parks
(http://www.colliergov.net/Index.aspx?page=2665)
(239) 252-4000

Boat Registration
(http://www.colliertax.com/vessel.html)
(239) 252-8176

Utilities and Garbage Collection

Florida Power & Light
(http://www.fpl.com/)
(239) 262-1322

Lee County Electric Cooperative
(https://www.lcec.net/)
(239) 995-2121

Collier County Water & Sewer
(http://www.colliergov.net/index.aspx?page=127)
(239) 252-2380

City of Naples Water & Sewer
(http://www.naplesgov.com/index.aspx?nid=128)
(239) 213-1800

City of Naples Garbage Collection
(http://www.naplesgov.com/index.aspx?nid=131)
(239) 213-4700

Collier County Garbage Collection
(http://www.colliergov.net/index.aspx?page=119)
(239) 252-2508

Cable Services

Comcast
(http://www.comcastoffers.com/florida/collier)
(239) 793-3577

Embarq
(http://www.moveutilities.com/embarq/)
(239) 596-6220

Bus Services

Collier Area Transit (CAT)
(http://www.colliergov.net/index.aspx?page=88)
(239) 596-7777

Greyhound
(https://www.greyhound.com/default.aspx)
(239) 774-5660

Business Assistance

Greater Naples Chamber of Commerce
(http://www.napleschamber.org)

SCORE
(http://www.naples.score.org/)
(239) 430-0081

Occupational Licensing
(http://www.colliergov.net/index.aspx?page=1004)
(239) 252-2477

Hospitals

NCH Downtown Naples Hospital
(http://www.nchmd.org)
(239) 436-5000

NCH North Collier Hospital
(http://www.nchmd.org)
(239) 552-7000

Physicians Regional Collier Campus
(http://www.physiciansregional.com)
(239) 354-6000

Physicians Regional Pine Ridge Campus
(http://www.physiciansregional.com)
(239) 348-4000

Police Non-Emergency

Naples Police Department
(http://www.naplesgov.com/index.aspx?NID=133)
(239) 213-4844

Education

Collier County Public Schools
(http://www.collier.k12.fl.us/)
(239) 377-0001

ACKNOWLEDGEMENTS

This book would not have come to be if not for Newt Barrett, friend and publisher, who somehow in his infinite wisdom believed I was the one to bring this idea to life.

Countless friends, colleagues and organizations helped make this book the comprehensive guide that it is.

Thank you to those who believed in the idea enough to contribute information and photos to the cause: PR pros, Cindy Dobyns, Ann Hughes, Teresa Morgenstern, Cyndee Woolley and E. Sue Huff; talented photographers, Scott Kelsey, Mike Dodge and Gareth Rockliffe; local experts, Jim Henderson, Artis Henderson, Cheryl Lampard and Ivan Seligman; Kali Horton of the Community Foundation of Collier County; Peg Ruby of Collier County Parks and Recreation; David Anderson and Frances Jones of FGCU; Phil Wood and Dottie Babcock of John R. Wood Realtors; Laura Rosen of the NCH Community Blood Center; and Robin Sheakley of Moving For Love.

Thank you to my husband, Weston, who showers me with confidence even in the midst of my doubt. He is always supportive of my choices and endures my moments of lunacy. Together we are unstoppable.

Thank you to dear friends, Cindy Dobyns, Soofia Khan-Bridgers, Karen Plunkett, Robin Mastandrea, Corey McCloskey, Bonnie Williams and Julie Littman, who enthusiastically cheered me on and were always happy to share their personal experiences. A special thanks to Soofia for letting me pick her brain about schools and kids while I fed her Christmas cookies hot from the oven.

Thank you to my best girls, Nicole Craven and Pam Reynolds, who have been by my side through every life adventure, including this one; your endless support means the world to me.

Thank you to my mom, who instilled in me a strong faith in the things we cannot see. I took a leap of faith with this project and I know she's above toasting my accomplishment (hopefully with a big slice of chocolate cake!). And to my dad, the strong, silent type, who nearly had a stroke when I shared with him my dream of becoming a writer. I know he was just worried for my future. I believe he's proud of how it all turned out.

Take it from me, a former Jersey girl, there's nothing better than waking every day to palm trees and sunshine. Even after all these years, I still have days when I can't believe this is my home. My hope is that you, too, discover Naples to be magical and that this book guides you in acclimating to life in what truly is paradise.

ABOUT THE AUTHOR

In February 2000, Alysia Shivers left the brutal cold and depressing gray skies of New Jersey and stepped off the plane at Southwest Florida International Airport into a sunshiny, 80-degree world. Alysia was in her mid-20s then and, until that moment, she had no desire to call Florida home.

Before the weekend ended, she was desperate to stay. In truth, Alysia was never cut out for snow, ice and near-zero temperatures. Five months later, she and her husband were Naples residents and today they can never imagine going back to the northeast.

Alysia is proof that you can have a professional career in Naples. Her degree in print journalism took her to The Registry Resort (now the Waldorf Astoria), where she was public relations manager, then on to Gulfshore Media, where she served as managing editor for *Gulfshore Life* and *Gulfshore Business* magazines. Alysia's writing skills eventually landed her at John R. Wood Realtors, where she started as publications director in the marketing department. More than seven years later, she left her position, which had evolved to e-marketing specialist, to pursue her entrepreneurial spirit as a Realtor with John R. Wood Realtors.

Today, Alysia devotes her time to marketing this fantastic place she calls home and helping others who are tired of those cold, gray days find their places in this beautiful beachside town.

Visit Alysia at

http://www.aroundtownwithalysia.com

Connect with her on Twitter

@alysh